Orion is Upside Down

Amy Kernahan was born and brought up on the Isle of Lewis in Scotland's Outer Hebrides, but is now an 'economic migrant' to the South East of England, where she works as an assembly, integration and test engineer for a company building small satellites in Guildford, Surrey. A fascination with technology led her to choose a career path that she believed would bring her to its cutting edge, gaining along the way a Masters in Aerospace Engineering from the University of Glasgow and studying for a time at the prestigious Ecole Nationale Supérieur de l'Aéronautique et de l'Espace in Toulouse. (She maintains that the reality is somewhat different and that whoever said the space industry is glamorous has never worked in it!) But her first love has always been the sea. *Orion is Upside Down* is her first book and is a sea story with almost as much ice as there is brine about it. Amy recounts the events and adventures of a journey to Antarctica and the sub-Antarctic Islands, drawing parallels and contrasts between the places she visits and the island she reluctantly calls home. Amy is a typical travel writer in that she insists that she is not a travel writer!

Orion is Upside Down

Amy Kernahan

Arena Books

First published in 2011 by Arena Books

Arena Books
6 Southgate Green
Bury St. Edmunds
IP33 2BL

www.arenabooks.co.uk

Distributed in America by Ingram International, One Ingram Blvd., PO Box
3006, La Vergne, TN 37086-1985, USA.

Amy Kernahan
  Orion is Upside Down
  1. Kernahan, Amy – Travel – Antarctica. 2. Kernahan, Jack -
  Travel – Antarctica. 3. Travel – Religious aspects.
  4. Spiritual life. 5. Antarctica – Description and travel.
  6. Shackleton, Ernest Henry, Sir, 1874-1922 – Tomb.
  I. Title
  919.8'9'04'092-dc22

ISBN 978-1-906791-75-9

BIC categories:- WTL, WTLP, 1MTS, WTHA, WTHX.

Printed & bound by Lightning Source UK

Cover design
by Jason Anscomb

Typeset in
Times New Roman

This book is printed on paper adhering to the Forest Stewardship Council™
(FSC®) mixed Credit FSC® C084699.

CONTENTS

LIST OF ILLUSTRATIONS
(Plates will be found between pages 76 and 77)

Plates 1
  (1) *Nordnorge* and MV *Isle of Lewis* in Stornoway Harbour
  (2) The May Revolution Monument in Buenos Aires
Plates 2
  (3) Mural in Ushuaia, arriving in the town from the airport
  (4) The Prison Train at Museo Maritimo y ex Presidio de Ushuaia
  (5) The author in the coach of the Prison Train
  (6) Transport Weekend Puky Body sign, Ushuaia
Plates 3
  (7) A large cruise ship and two Argentinian naval vessels, Ushuaia
  (8) One of the trains that operates the End of The World Railway, Ushuaia
Plates 4
  (9) The author photographed filming their passage around Cape Horn
  (10)   Jack Kernahan preparing to go ashore
  (11)   Passengers go ashore from a Polar Cirkle inflatable
Plates 5
  (12)   *Nordnorge* at Niko Harbour

List of Illustrations

Stornoway

The hills of the mainland. If you can see them, it's going to rain. If you can't, it is raining. Welcome to my island.

The Isle of Lewis lies on the edge of the Old World. It is the largest of the chain of islands that form the Outer Hebrides, separated from mainland Scotland to the east by 50 miles of a particularly nasty little sea called the Minch. Stand on the west coast and look out to the horizon and the next stop is Canada.

It's a Saturday afternoon and the hills of the mainland are not visible. We're in a coffee house with dark green signage. This is before a certain Seattle-based coffee house chain opened its first establishment in the UK, but in the years that follow, Starbucks' livery will always remind me of Merchant's. There must be about eight or ten of us, but folk are appearing, disappearing and then reappearing in such a way that it's difficult to tell. The barista, unaffectionately known, to us at least, as the Hag Behind the Counter, is watching us like one of the witches of folk-lore, fixing us with the Evil Eye and looking for the slightest reason to throw us out. But we give her none, and at least three of us have a coffee in front of us at any one time. I'm gazing around me at the framed posters and prints on the walls. I do this every time I'm in here. I never tire of it. Old posters advertising tea and coffee from the days of Empire when importing them from its far-flung reaches was a romantic and adventurous undertaking. Prints of elegant tea clippers, sleek thoroughbreds of the sea, some of them with five masts, the most magnificent spread of canvas imaginable. Oh, if I'd lived then…

My grandfather ran away to sea. He lied about his age and joined the Navy at the outbreak of the First World War. Fought in the Battle of Jutland. The sea is in my blood and bones. Growing up on an island off the coast of an island, an island nation that once 'ruled the waves' binds me to it, cruel mistress though it is.

A young woman from the next table leans across to us. There is a large rucksack leaning against her chair. My guess is she's just come off the ferry after being tossed around in the Minch for two and three-quarter hours.

'Excuse me,' she asks, 'but what do you do on Saturday afternoons in Stornoway?'

She's not a tourist; she's a traveller. Try to see a place the way the 'real' people there see it. Even if that place is Stornoway.

Katie, Joanne and I exchange glances.

'Err…'

'This,' says Katie.

You can see why I wanted to leave.

Merchant's Coffee House isn't there anymore. It's become a Chinese restaurant painted in the tackiest blue and gold. It's eight years since that rainy Saturday afternoon...

CHAPTER 1
Buenos Aires

'To adventure!'

Across the table, my travelling companion added 'Sláinte!'

Ah, you can take the Scots out of Scotland, but you'll never take Scotland out of the Scots.

Setting his glass down, blue eyes gazed into it as though seeing the possibilities of the days – weeks – to come sparkling in the dark liquid, bright eyes set in a nut-brown face, whipped by wind and rain more than kissed by sun, eyes that shone with fierce intelligence and a mischievous wit.

A crown, not so much of silver but more like pewter, encircling the top of his head was all that belied his otherwise youthful appearance and gave any suggestion that he was closer to sixty than fifty. It was a crown of the wisdom gained only by living in a world harsh as well as kind, rather than one of bright and delicate finery.

Jack Kernahan is my fellow explorer, trusted utterly and loved completely. He is my teacher in life and instructor in learning, my mentor, my comrade and my friend.

Oh, yes, and he's my dad as well.

And what had brought me here, not just to this restaurant in Buenos Aires, further away from home than I had ever been, but to this point where I was about to begin a journey of the soul that I had been moving inexorably towards for years, he had seen it all.

I wonder what he saw when he looked into the scintillating darkness of that glass.

I was six years old when I first laid eyes upon the most beautiful thing I had ever seen. The fuzzy images were so dim that colour was imperceptible, picked out only by the searchlights of a tiny submersible two and a half miles below the surface of the Atlantic Ocean.

What bound us together I do not know. It was as though the iron atoms in my blood and those in her hull had known each other in the heart of the star that exploded to form our solar system.

She was handsome, she was pretty.

She was the belle of Belfast City.

Her name was *Titanic*.

To a child fascinated by machinery, she was the Figure of Beatrice. And like Bice di Folco Portinari she died young.

Dante found ice at the very centre of Hell.

Krakens, Sirens, even the Old Testament Leviathan were diminished before these diabolical creations that had the arrogance and contempt of virtue to clothe themselves in white. The beast that came up out of the sea in St John's vision on the island of Patmos was made, in my childlike theology, of ice. And the authority given to that beast by the dragon, its propensity to sink, nay, *slay* ships, was in that theology given to it by the devil himself.[i]

I first saw an iceberg when I circumnavigated the island of Spitsbergen in the High Arctic in the summer of 2002. It didn't look evil. It was alone, holding court in this fjord with its minions of brash and growlers around it. It was silent. It was serene. It was *blue*. Then, anchoring at a respectful distance, we got into Zodiac inflatables and crept across the surface of the fjord, littered with ice, towards it. The silence had weight, pressing down upon us and the helmsman coaxed our little boat cautiously around it, as though the iceberg were a sleeping giant and one lap of the water against its flanks, one mis-placed sound, would wake it. I believe we did wake it, but not to wrath. We woke it to indifference. Chilled, arrogant indifference. Like an anti-sun it radiated cold, reaching out to touch my face in a caress which made my skin crawl as much from revulsion as from the cold. It was a touch that would never leave me. I changed my mind. It didn't *look* evil; it *was* evil.

He tipped his glass forward a little, light from the candle in the centre of the table caught in the liquid darkness…

There had been a discovery of great historical significance. Or, a relic from my childhood that could potentially serve to embarrass me at family get-togethers for the foreseeable future (particularly as I had managed to mix up a transit of Venus with a solar eclipse. When you learn more about me you will understand why this is terribly embarrassing). A cardboard folder had been unearthed containing essays, pictures and such creations clearly produced by a child's hand on the subject of Captain James Cook. Or, more accurately, the subject of Captain James Cook's discovery of Australia. When the class had been asked what they thought of the subject the author of the newly uncovered work had said that she was bored of hearing 'the same story over and over again' and would have rather heard more about Antarctica.

'The part I enjoyed most,' I had written, for your author now was that author then, of the otherwise deeply unsatisfying project, 'was drawing the chalk pictures of the Antarctic.' And there it was, a rather smudged representation of chalky icebergs, a sailing vessel edging its way between them unharmed, as though by some sort of pictorial voodoo its escape could bring some sort of justice upon the perpetrator of that crime of April 1912 long since melted.

The one thing I had learned from that project that I considered of any value was that icebergs lived in the South as well as the North.

We seek a St George for every dragon, a Vidar for every Fenrir. But in the absence of saints and demi-gods there was still a man who was, for me, a natural hero.

Sir Ernest Shackleton.

A knight in windproof Burberry.

The man they called the Boss.

And the ice chose the wrong man to pick a fight with.

For when it had stripped them of ship, shelter and supplies, he led his crew out of that frozen Hell and left them on edge of it while he went to seek rescue, a voyage in an open boat across an open ocean that would define the Heroic Age of Polar exploration.

'Abandon hope all ye who enter here,' is inscribed upon the lintel of Dante's Hell-mouth[ii]; it has been said, when comparing the qualities of the polar pioneers, 'When no hope is left get on your knees and pray for Shackleton.'[iii]

> Forward! Henceforth there's but one will for two,
> Thou master, thou leader and thou lord...[iv]

That was why I was sitting here in a restaurant in Buenos Aires toasting 'Adventure' with Coca Cola. There was no penguin 'dressed for dinner'[1] wandering around on the table (and for that I was truly thankful), but I was about to set out from South America and 'enter on that savage path'[v] across the Drake Passage and down the Antarctic Peninsula. How far we got would depend on the whims of the pack ice, and in this the southern autumn it was already creeping northward.

Our return north would follow to an extent Shackleton's return journey after the loss of his ship, *Endurance*, during the Imperial Trans-Antarctic Expedition of 1914-16, albeit starting from the other side of the Peninsula. We would pass Elephant Island, where the crew of *Endurance* awaited rescue for four and a half months while Shackleton and five others took the cutter, named *James Caird* after one of the expedition's benefactors, and sailed for South Georgia. Two landings were planned for South Georgia, one a visit to Stromness, the one-time whaling community from which Shackleton was able to raise help for his stranded men, and the other to Grytviken, the 'capital' of South Georgia, its seat of authority as a British Overseas Territory.

The 'Shackleton Trail' complete, we would then spend two days in the Falkland Islands, one in Stanley, the other at Westpoint Island, before sailing

---

[1] Possibly apocryphal moment from Channel 4's mini-series *Shackleton* when a penguin was placed on the table during a dinner party in Buenos Aires before the *Endurance* departed for

once again for Argentina, disembarking at Buenos Aires.

***

To be delayed by snow was not an auspicious start to a journey to the Antarctic. The effect of the substance on transportation networks is not limited to the British railways. The snow had fallen in Madrid and I imagine that there, no snow would have been 'the right kind of snow.'

The British contingent of the expedition was separated before the adventure even began. The flight that was to have taken us to Madrid (there to connect to Buenos Aires) had been cancelled and its passengers divided up between two others. (Extra passengers, extra baggage, extra weight; extra weight, extra fuel; extra fuel, extra cost...) The allotment of passengers to alternative flights was completely random. We didn't know it at the time, but we had a fifty per cent chance of getting into a spot of bother.

We took possession of our new boarding cards and watched our luggage glide away on the conveyor belt. I marvelled at the workings of the Machine that allowed these objects to disappear into the internal infrastructure of the airport and reappear on a conveyor belt half-way across the world (or half way across the country if one is taking a domestic flight – it's equally amazing, I think) to miraculously be reunited with their owners. Hopefully. All miracles require a little bit of faith.

We were particularly grateful to watch Dad's suitcase drift off, after startling the scales into a blinking frenzy with its weight. Dad was very proud of the 'Heavy' label it had been awarded once before and insisted that it remain attached. The suitcase, one of those ones you could hide a body in, had gone lame. It had been to the Antarctic before, it was on that journey that it had gained its 'Heavy' accolade, and decided that it didn't want to go back. It ground to a halt on the footbridge of Guildford Station, the axel of its wheels completely seized, and refused to go a yard further of its own volition. It had been wrestled on and off modes of transport from there to the airport and we were now delighted to see it disappear and become Someone Else's Problem for a few hours.

By the way, I happen to believe the credentials of the most famous miracle worker there ever was.

We arrived in Madrid on a flight that should have left Heathrow three hours before we arrived at that illustrious airport. I hate Heathrow. And being trapped there by weather in another part of the continent, a part of the continent considered by the UK at large to be a meteorological El Dorado, was not helping any negative associations I have with the place.

The woman at the check-in desk had been very apologetic that she couldn't give us seats together on our new flight. But as we were about to spend sixteen days on a ship together that really wasn't important. Dad said as much, adding genially, 'Just so long as we're on the same flight!' Ah, the clichéd true word spoke in jest. If we had been on different flights, we would have had a one hundred per cent chance that one of us would have got into a spot of bother.

I couldn't even see Dad from where I was sitting. I was in the middle of the row of three and consoled myself that by my suffering it, someone else who was less physically compatible with such spaces didn't have to (I had once been the butt of much ribbing from the rest of my group travelling back from Houston on a 747, when I was given the seat next to the emergency exit over the wing – it was deemed cosmically unjust that the shortest person on the plane got the seat with the most leg-room).

'It's a Norwegian icebreaker.'

Or, 'IT'S A NORWEGIAN ICEBREAKER.'

The voice, loud and English, boomed out above the fast and lilting Spanish voices of moderate volume that, along with the ever-present hum of the aeroplane's engines, formed the ambient noise in the cabin. I twisted and tried to peer between the headrests. I wondered if he was headed for the Antarctic as well. It seemed a reasonable guess. I hoped he wouldn't be disappointed. *Nordnorge* isn't an icebreaker. She's ice-class-C, structurally reinforced and 'built for ice conditions' one might say, of which there are plenty in her native Norway, but she's not a breaker.

I decided that I didn't mind looking like a meerkat for a moment in order to satisfy my curiosity and popped my head up above the expanse of hair, interspersed with the odd baseball cap. The man who had spoken was *three* rows behind me.

Madrid was worse than Heathrow. At least there it had been only the Spanish flights that had the 'Delayed-delayed-cancelled-delayed' mantra running down their departure boards. As our flight from London had got later and later (we were all aboard and sitting on the apron for over an hour before we were given permission to even taxi to the runway) there was a fear that we would miss our connection to Buenos Aires. But we needn't have worried. It had joined the list of the Delayed.

There is a strange creature that has been sighted in Madrid Airport. It is thought not to be native to these parts, but migrating through on its way from somewhere in Africa to unknown but diverse destinations in the northern hemisphere. Dad had seen one the last time he travelled through the Airport. As an intrepid traveller returning from Terra Incognita, he was surely in the frame of mind to expect such wonders.

'I couldn't believe it,' he said when he told the grand tale. 'I have absolutely no idea how it got on the aeroplane. But this guy had a six-foot wooden giraffe under his arm!'

I had been on the lookout for this creature with the same childlike curiosity with which I had once scrutinised the surface of Loch Ness as we drove alongside it in the car, and was met with similar disappointment.

Around midnight, the departure boards, which had indifferently reported 'Delayed' for the last several hours, flashed green and directed us to a gate.

'Oh,' said Dad flatly.

He knew it. It was about as far away as was possible without leaving the terminal building. But we were on the move, and the hunt was on. Maybe on this epic trek I would catch a glimpse of the fabled six-foot wooden giraffe.

The gate was dark. Maybe this is good, I thought. Maybe they like the dark. I spotted Loud Englishman. It was probably he who had frightened away all the giraffes. I pointed him out to Dad, whispering in case I further disturbed them (well, not really, but there is something that compels us to whisper in dark, quiet places and I have no idea what it is, so I'll put it down to the giraffes on this occasion). But the lack of activity was a little disconcerting.

Then the departure boards, or the people operating them, decided to liven up the nightshift and have a bit of fun with the passengers of the Delayed Twenty-Three Forty Iberian Airlines Flight to Buenos Aires. I can just picture them sniggering away at the CCTV screens as we followed each other from gate to gate for the next hour or so like hapless sheep on a surreal nocturnal treasure hunt (I have to admit, it's the sort of thing I would find funny). But as far as I was concerned, I was stalking the legendary six-foot wooden giraffe, and if I roamed this dim wilderness of wide, empty airport companionways long enough I would surely come across one.

I was very tired. And when I get tired I get silly.

I was so tired that after we had finally boarded our flight (from the first gate we had been directed to when our adventure into the unknown of Madrid Airport had begun, and had so disappointingly failed to yield any sightings of giraffes, wooden and six feet tall or otherwise) I was only able to briefly enthuse about getting a ride on an A340 before succumbing.

'I slept through take-off!' I exclaimed as I popped back into consciousness, roused by the cabin crew who were now distributing the ubiquitous trays of things mostly edible but entirely unidentifiable.

'I know you did!' Dad sounded equally surprised. I usually give a running commentary to anyone who'll listen on every aerodynamic action on the wings of an aircraft during take-off or landing. Even if no-one's listening, I'll enthuse about it anyway. I once *saw* the double helical vortex shed from the wing tip of the plane, formed from the water vapour of the clouds through which we were descending. The guy sitting next to me really couldn't have cared less, but I was elated to see with my own eyes what hereto had just been an idealised diagram in my aerodynamics textbook. All the mathematics that so poetically described flight were not just scientific facts, but *true*. (See, I've just done it, and we're not even *on* an aeroplane.)

Airports take the romance out of travelling. Stornoway has a modern airport (no, it's not 'the one where they land on the beach,' that's Barra), although until a few years ago it was just a glorified Port-a-cabin, but I far prefer to arrive in my birthplace by ferry, though she is a simple, functional ship devoid of any great beauty. With air travel you sort of drop in from the sky.

Thus I had no expectations about Buenos Aires airport, just accepted that it would be my first sight of Argentina and that it would not be much different from any other airport I had travelled through – tourists in shorts you wouldn't dare wear any place you might be recognised, businessmen in perfectly tailored suits, obviously locals because the heat was causing them no visible discomfort, children riding on trolleys despite, or maybe because of signs in a multitude of languages telling them not to, and mountains of suitcases rising above the dark polished floor like volcanic islands peeping out of the sea. Or icebergs…

What I certainly hadn't expected was a cry of 'Harry Potter!'

I was still dressed for Guildford in February, feeling a little silly in heavy leather jacket, beanie hat and maroon and gold scarf. The scarf is usually mistaken for Motherwell FC, but it was to this accessory that the customs officer, a woman so small she seemed to vanish in her booth, which itself wasn't exactly large, was pointing excitedly, having identified it, correctly, as a replica Gryffindor house scarf.

Perhaps it wasn't so surprising. The adventures of the boy wizard have been translated into more than sixty languages, including Latin and Ancient Greek. (The Scottish Gaelic edition is on its way. Dead languages obviously take priority over terminally ill ones.)

Our luggage was in no hurry to show itself. Of course the Airbus A340, about which I had managed to briefly enthuse before conking out, is a huge plane, but our bags really were taking their time. I was gloomily concluding that someone's bag has to be last off when a woman approached us from the direction of the Customer Services desk. Possibly on hearing our non-Spanish voices, she asked us,

'Were you on the flight from London?'

It was not a time to be pedantic about there being more than one flight from London that connected with the Buenos Aires flight, although we might have saved ourselves some anxiety if we had been.

'Yes,' Dad replied.

(Still no sign of our luggage.)

'Some of the bags from that flight have been left behind.'

'In Madrid?'

'In London.'

I studied aeronautical engineering, and thus gained some, shall we say… insight into how some airlines operate. Aviation fuel is expensive, and if a plane is overloaded not all the baggage will make it on board. It costs them less to send the baggage on later and pay the passengers compensation. The flight that the woman was referring to was obviously one of the two that had taken the passengers from the cancelled one.

I wasn't sure I really believed it. There was so much activity and no obvious organisation and reclaim carrousels with completely random points of origin right next to each other that it would be very easy for someone to miss something somewhere and start the rumour mill grinding.

Dad thanked her with a tired sigh and we picked our way around the archipelago of suitcases to Customer Services. The woman there, a slight emission of urgency escaping from beneath an otherwise calm demeanour that made me start to think there might be some truth to the story, scrutinised our luggage deposit receipts.

'Are you certain they are not there?' A nearly-but-not-quite Spanish accent, born of the differences in diction between the Spanish of Spain and that spoken here, I hypothesised.

We weren't certain. The carousel was still conveying large numbers of bags, and it was only a couple of minutes after returning to our post that Dad's wounded monster appeared. He hauled it off the belt in great relief at having found it, even in its deteriorating condition. But where was mine?

I spotted it at the base of one of the suitcase islands, an eighty-five litre rucksack forming a dark grey cliff descending to the polished black sea. I picked it up. As I was negotiating my way awkwardly around the obstacles with it a middle aged man with what might in detective literature be described as a fierce moustache – although really it was the face behind it that was fierce – launched himself towards me shouting at me in excited Spanish. I pointed to the identity tag, demanding of him in equally excited English, 'Is your name Kernahan?' I had just come off a delayed thirteen-hour overnight flight and the South American heat was beginning to work its way under my collar already, and I was in no mood for being falsely accused of theft by a random Argentinean, who would not have been terribly impressed to get home and find the bag full of women's underwear and cold weather gear for a very short person. The three-quarters-of-a-grand-sterling's worth of photographic equipment might have made up for it though. The man humphed and shrugged in a way that made me think he might have some French blood in him. But I didn't hear the words 'Lo siento.'

We man-hauled our luggage out into the sun, as the trolleys needed coins to unlock them and we had none. Maybe it was psychological, but the sun seemed much stronger now that we were in the southern hemisphere. Or maybe it really was *hot*. Europe was still in winter's grip and we were on the way to the Antarctic, cold bread to a hot sandwich that I could have done without. On the tarmac next to the bus which would take us to our hotel the British contingent was united for the first time. But something was not quite right.

There seemed to be a rather high people-to-luggage ratio. It hadn't been a rumour generated by the apparent disorderliness of Buenos Aires Airport. Nineteen bags had been left in Madrid.

There had been a bomb alert while we had been retrieving our luggage. Nobody seemed to have noticed.

***

On the pages of the primary school atlases Edinburgh, Cardiff and Belfast were always marked by little red squares to distinguish them as 'capital cities' even though this was in the days before devolution. But London was marked by a splat on the page following approximately the contours of the M25. By similar representation, Buenos Aires ought to be the size of Wales. Its urban sprawl actually covers 1,500 square miles, not quite large enough to lose a small country in, but at 859 square miles, if the Isle of Lewis wandered off you'd never find it again.

It had been called an 'orientation tour.' What it amounted to was being driven around a complex series of one-way systems, to which the coach only grudgingly adhered. The major landmarks of Downtown Buenos Aires were pointed out to us as we passed them at a speed which left us craning our necks in the hope that we would remember where they were in relation to each other. And the sun was in the wrong place.

I remember someone I met in California who had just come back from Australia trying to convince me that the sun rises in the west in the southern hemisphere. That only happens on Venus. (They-with-a-capital-T think it's upside down.) But I'll let her off because the sun does appear to travel the other way across the sky. You just need to remember that it's in the north.

King Harry (Shakespeare's Henry V) likens a 'good heart' to the sun 'because he holds his course true and never falters.' Perhaps what often seems strange and contrary to nature may still be the true course of a good heart, we're just looking at it through the lens of what we perceive as the natural order. But we are not to blame for the mistake. It wasn't my fault I was born in the northern hemisphere.

An assessment of the damage to Dad's case after we arrived at the hotel led to the conclusion that it was terminal. So with the objective of procuring another we set off into the mid-afternoon heat, our disorientating orientation tour still fresh in our memories – we would probably have been better off had it not – and following a map that on occasions we both thought was upside down.

There is a disturbing abundance of pink in Buenos Aires. Not only do numerous public buildings sport the colour but the Presidential Palace, as well as its official title La Casa de Gobierno, also goes by the name La Casa Rosada, the Pink Palace. This to me sounded more like an establishment one might find in Soho, and the baby-blue of the national flag wasn't helping.

There are two explanations offered for the travesty of decking out the seat of government of the Argentine nation thus. One is that it was for the purpose of diplomacy, by mixing the colours, red and white, of the two opposing political parties. The other is that the original paint was mixed with cows' blood to prevent damage from humidity. I don't know a great deal about the thermal properties of cows' blood, it doesn't feature as a material ever used in aeronautical engineering, but I don't see how it can protect against humidity. And as I rather like the idea of easing 'tensions' between our own Labour and Conservative Parties by painting the Palace of Westminster purple, my vote is for the former. But its being idealistic, a gesture striving for political peace, and the latter being purely practical, the cows' blood theory is probably more likely. Or less unlikely.

But right now, if it were true that cows' blood really does have protective thermal properties, I would quite willingly have lathered myself in the stuff.

Buenos Aires was named after the patron saint of the Spanish sailors who first landed in the vicinity, St Mary of the Good Air. I wasn't sure that she was blessing the city that bears her name right now. The air was hot. Air that exceeds human body temperature can never, in my book, be good. I'm Scottish. We don't cope well with heat, receiving so little of it in our natural habitat.

The city is full of the nearly-but-not-quite familiarity that globalisation has brought. Billboards advertise soft drinks and mobile phones, but with subtle differences in the artwork that tells you you're not in the UK. But I did a double take when I saw a girl in a phone box in a Manchester United shirt with a large '7' and 'Beckham' printed on the back. (Like many of the other infiltrations it was a little behind, David Beckham had already been sold to Real Madrid.) But there was no real reason why I should have. Like many kids growing up on football in the Eighties I idolised Diego Maradonna, 'hand of God' or no 'hand of God.' Indeed, particularly as a Scottish kid growing up on football in that decade, *because* of the Appendage of the Deity, which had put England out of the 1986 World Cup. I'd somehow never really connected him with the country that invaded the Falklands, despite the outright hostility that accompanies all England-Argentina internationals. But in football, for the Scot, there is no greater enemy than the English.

An excuse for footballing bigotries is not the only remaining vestige of the animosity between the factions of the Falklands conflict. It is impossible to change sterling directly to pesos.

Our travel agent boasted that they could obtain any currency in the world. Except pesos.

Although in large towns and cities the US dollar is accepted, we were planning an expedition in Ushuaia that would take us outside the town boundaries, and we were not taking any chances. Local currency would at least be more polite, even if the infiltration of the US dollar had reached these parts.

Had it not been so hot I would have passed a pleasant three quarters of an hour on a bench near the bank where Dad went to get pesos. The voice of my thermodynamics lecturer came back to me, droning on about how the hotter fluid (in this case the air) would pass heat to the cooler fluid (my blood). Then I thought of turbine blades, and Doc Green's diagrams of them on the blackboard, ever worsening as the lecture went on, coolant pumping through them beneath the surface. The perspiration on my skin? The human machine…

Dad at last obtained his pesos. The bank would not exchange directly from sterling, so he had had to change some of our precious US dollars, the currency that would be used on board ship (despite the ship and her operating line being Norwegian) and would be required to pay our airport tax that would allow us to leave the country when we were on our way home.

The currency confusion did not end there. It appears that the peso is prefixed with the dollar sign.

'Where do you start looking in a city like this for a luggage shop?'

We had set off in happy optimism that we would be able to find anything we were looking for, even if we went in completely the wrong direction a couple of times (but that was the city's fault for being south of the equator) and spoke no Spanish. But fortune favours the bold (or naïve) and, even in a city 'centre' of 700 square miles (remember the area of Lewis!)…

'Look,' I said. 'Samsonite.'

Like Coca-Cola, Harry Potter and Manchester United, here was another familiar name, emblazoned with its associated logo above a shop door. We went inside, grateful for the air-conditioning that hit us in the face as we did so. The woman in the shop who spoke excellent English with a strange accent that was a mixture of the Spanish dialect spoken in Argentina and American, was eager to help, and we spent a good twenty minutes examining the wheels of a veritable parade of cases.

'This feels fairly solid.'

'The axle's exposed.'

'What about… I think the wheels are hollow.'

'Hollow? Oh, that one looks good.'

'No, the wheels are shoogley.'

The shop assistant might have spoken excellent English, but not Scottish. The word earned us a dubious look.

At last a decision was reached and a large, light but solid case with a $300 price tag was purchased using a Master Card as our supply of dollars had been depleted already by the peso palaver. The shop assistant had been delighted that we'd chosen it, and the shop was a Samsonite retailer and though the case was of a make we'd never heard of we trusted that they were generally suppliers of quality. That and the '$300' convinced us that we had made a good purchase. After all, you get what you pay for.

CHAPTER 2
Ushuaia

It was more like getting on a school bus that getting on a plane.
  'Andreas, ich kan nicht du finden.'
  'There's Shirley, over by the emergency exit.'
  'Hey, Chuck! I've saved a seat for ya!'
All regardless of whether Andreas wanted to be found, or whether Chuck, who probably preferred to be called Charles, wanted a seat saved for him. In all likelihood they'd become sworn brothers at the Salsa Night the previous evening, and from now on one half of each pairing would spend the rest of the trip trying to avoid the other. How easy was that going to be on a ship in the Antarctic? Perhaps Shirley was already taking precautions.

We hadn't bothered with the salsa. As far as I'm concerned, salsa is something you dip tortilla chips in. And is far superior to guacamole.

As the plane took off, I was quietly relieved to be leaving Buenos Aires. Dad had flooded his bathroom, and left the carcass of his old suitcase in his room with a big label reading 'Please destroy.' The two incidents were unrelated. His new not-Samsonite, 300 'dollar' price-tag suitcase was safely in the hold, which was more than could be said for a certain nineteen others that should have started from Heathrow. The missing cases had failed to materialise overnight, and now their owners were counting on them arriving in Buenos Aires in time for a second flight to Ushuaia chartered for that afternoon. At least Dad's had made it to Argentina, even if it had been the luggage equivalent of an animated corpse.

In the free-for-all boarding I'd been able to get my favourite seat over the wing, but I was still able to see the sky-scape around us. The last time Dad had taken an internal flight in Argentina, he'd said that the plane had had to flap its little wings to get over the mountains. Our geriatric 737 wasn't doing much better. The wing was bending and flexing, the aerodynamic forces acting upon it tweaked by the high-rise geology over which we were flying. In a way, it *was* flapping. And I'm sure the plane was flying far closer to the mountains than Boeing ever intended. In my mind's eye I saw a map of Argentina superimposed on the carpet of mountain-tops below and in front of us, a red line creeping southwards to the sound of that famous theme tune – da-da-d-daa, da-da-daaa – over them.

Descent, of course, brought us closer.

I don't normally have any problems with my ears on aircraft. As part of the training for a parabolic flight I once made, I and my three colleagues were sealed in a hyperbaric chamber and the pressure was dropped to the equivalent of 30, 000 feet, so low that we had to wear oxygen masks. But despite having no difficulty whatsoever with a simulated ascent and descent to and from jumbo jet cruising altitude coming down through those mountains in that old Boeing played havoc with my inner ears as the air was slowly bled back in to the cabin.

Knowing what makes your ears pop in a pressurised aircraft doesn't make it any less uncomfortable when they don't.

I swallowed and swallowed, pinched my nose and blew, then tried following the advice of the old British Airways advert and took big gulps and thought of Des Lyman. Nothing.

'Well, here we are then,' said Dad as the reverse thrust of the engines ceased and the plane trundled forward towards the terminal building, tottering a little as it was buffeted now by a stiff, high altitude wind instead of the forces generated by its own lift.

I barely heard him.

The descent through the mountains had made me go partially deaf.

***

The bus laboured asthmatically up the hill. The wind whipped us as we staggered out, making it slightly difficult to breathe and leaving us in a similar condition to the bus. This assault struck me as a little unfair – the wind had quite enough air of its own without stealing any more from out of our very lungs. 'The wind blows wherever it pleases. We hear its sound but we cannot tell where it comes from of where it is going.'[vi] Maybe the wind is made of the stolen breath of people who gaze upon amazing things in amazing places, and that's why such things 'take one's breath away.' I certainly prefer that to its being nothing more than moving air flowing from regions of high to low atmospheric pressure. The wooden building that was the purpose of the trundle up this hill that had so distressed our poor bus was not, in itself, 'breath-taking.' But this was the first building of the settlement that would bear the name Ushuaia.

Appearing slightly incongruous in what one might have called the front garden of this historical piece of otherwise unremarkable architecture there stood an aging aeroplane, nevertheless looking like it was ready to take off and adding to the Indiana Jones feel of the place.

Looking over the shoulder of the aeroplane, I saw our ship dominating the harbour of the most southerly town in the world, a town squeezed out along the coast, trapped by the mountains behind and the sea in front, all grown from the seed of the unassuming building on this windy hill. Thriving on staple industries of electrical appliance manufacture and similar, modern Ushuaia is a world away from the gentle farmers, growing their grains and keeping their goats, who were its first citizens. And how far removed were they from what the native populace had been a mere fifty years before that, nomadic hunters and fishermen who 'here at the world's end... had lived unmolested to that day.'[2] Although less brutal than the conquest to which those words originally referred, that of the might of Rome over the island that would one day be known as Great Britain, the 'conquest' of this corner of Patagonia was more complete. Two thousand years later, the Celts are still to be found in Scotland. Within less than a hundred years, the Yaghan race had all but died out. The unforeseen revenge for the unproven theft of a small boat was the gradual destruction of a culture from the inside out.

Despite the abundance of the colour in its capital city, on the world map Argentina, not even its curly little tail, had never been pink. The British conquest of Tierra del Fuego had not been imperial; it had been religious. And the testimony to its final, successful advance lay behind me.

The house, which had just suddenly found itself playing second fiddle to an elderly aeroplane, was that built by Thomas Bridges when he established a Christian community here in 1870. He is probably the only evangelist whose name brings up adverts for accessories for children's model railways when Googled.

It had begun by a twist of fate more that forty years before, when four Yaghans were taken hostage by the Master of His Britannic Majesty's Ship *Beagle* for the return of one of the ship's boats, allegedly stolen by the natives. (This was indeed the same *Beagle* made famous by Charles Darwin, although the naturalist was not aboard at that time.) The stolen boat was not returned and the four Yaghans were given ridiculous names (Fuegia Basket, Jimmy Button, Boat Memory and... wait for it ... York Minster) and taken to England. They were entrusted to the care of one Reverend William Wilson, who no doubt seeing this as an opportunity to fulfil prophecy of Acts 1:8: 'Ye shall be witnesses unto me...unto the uttermost part of the earth,' had them instructed in the ways of the Gospel then sent them back to their people to spread the Good News. They returned to Tierra del Fuego aboard the *Beagle*. This time, Charles Darwin was aboard. These new initiates to Christianity were taking it back to their people on the same voyage that would cast the first true doubt over the concept of Creation.

It failed miserably, and, on occasion, tragically.

And yet they persisted with their rituals and ceremonies, utterly alien to the Yaghan, the People. How were they to know that during the first church service to be held in the land, a simple gathering of the crew of the ship that had arrived in their waters, these strangers were only offering praises and thanks to their benevolent God for bringing them safely across the sea from England? How were they to know that they were not calling down the wrath of the gods

---

[2] Refers to a speech allegedly made by Calgacus, the Caledonian chieftain, before the Battle of Mons Graupius as recorded by Tacitus, the original Scottish battle-cry of 'Freedom!' The Caledonians lost. The story of our lives throughout history.

upon the people of the land they intended to invade? The Yaghans massacred almost the entire congregation, leaving only one survivor.

'And I only am escaped alone to tell thee.'[vii]

Tierra del Fuego had created its first Christian martyrs.

The Yaghans naturally feared retribution, which never came. Perhaps it was this, the practical demonstration of the forgiveness preached in the Gospel, rather than trying to change a people's way of thinking with examples of 'here's one I made earlier' that made the difference. Perhaps this was why George Despard and his adopted son Thomas Bridges, who took over the seemingly terminal calling of ministering to the Yaghans, succeeded where his predecessors had failed.

The evangelisation of Patagonia had begun with ignorant arrogance, the re-education of four young people with the intention of having them show their people this better way of life, injecting them back into their society like a virus. A virus for which the immune system of this people's culture was too strong. Only when one of these intruders showed them what is at the heart of the Christian Gospel – forgiveness, God's forgiveness of Man, Man's forgiveness of each other – was that Gospel truly carried 'to the uttermost part of the earth.'

Ushuaia, named by the first British colonists after the name the Yaghan people themselves gave the area, means 'Inner Harbour to Westward.' Quite un-romantic when placed alongside the magnificent 'Land of Fire' in which it lies.

When those first western explorers sailed into these waters and saw smoke rising from the landmass it must have fitted well with what they might expect to find at the end of the world, in the absence of the ocean cascading down an infinite abyss in an endless waterfall.

The 'Land of Fire' is indeed aptly named. The Yaghans seemed to have a bit if a *thing* about fire, treating it almost as a sort of family pet. They never let their fires go out, and even *carried it with them in their canoes* when they went on extended hunting trips. Most seamen will tell you that fire at sea is one of the worst disasters that can befall a ship. I would, of course, like to nominate another. It has symmetry, the equals and opposites of nature that are necessary to define each other. Ice and fire, a ship's greatest enemies, yet when they collide and do battle they annihilate each other and become the element for which ships are created. Fire melts ice becomes water puts out fire. Were the Yaghans crazy? Or did they just understand that if one has the correct respect for something, even something so dangerous, one need not fear it?

That little house on a windy hill stands alone, unoccupied, its guard-dog aircraft a few yards away. Nothing else remains of that first little community except its name.

Across the water is Ushuaia proper, grown out of an Argentinean penal colony. The missionaries and preachers are all gone, but the legacy of thieves, murderers and political dissidents remains.

In Ushuaia, the Gospel may have been preached 'to the uttermost part of the Earth,' but the meek have not inherited it. There was no return to Eden here.

But the name survives, perhaps because those first pioneers did not impose their own upon it, but used instead the name given by the native people, the people to whom this land belonged. The Yaghan are all but consigned to history by white-man's disease and intermarriage with other peoples. Man is as the grass of the field, but the land endures, for now, and with it the name given to it by its own people, even if they are no more.

The prison, which formed the keystone of this penal colony appears to have no name other than 'Presidio de Ushuaia' – Ushuaia Prison. Perhaps this was Argentina's first territorial response to a British presence in the vicinity. That area of Patagonia was at that time 'unclaimed' by any sovereign power, or any republic for that matter. One could put an even more cynical head on and suppose that Argentina adopted Britain's own method for rapid colonisation, as demonstrated in Australia, our own administration of justice with dubious motives used against us. And telling of the sentence of the prisoners, transportation and hard labour, is a railway, known simply as the Prison Railway, built by the prisoners themselves, to ferry them each day to and from the forest surrounding the Inner Harbour to Westward. There they were put to work felling trees for use in the construction of the town that was growing up around the place of their incarceration and exile.

That railway still exists.

With 20/20 rear-view vision, it was a really stupid thing to do. Fate protects fools, little children and ships named *Enterprise*. Use a process of elimination to decide which category we fell into. (The name of our ship was *Nordnorge*, which is not Norwegian for 'Enterprise.')

I can only remember ever once being annoyed with my dad and that was when he got us lost halfway up a mountain just outside Bergen. Even this wouldn't have been that much of a problem if we hadn't had to catch a plane that afternoon. But leaping into a taxi and heading off into the wilds that push Ushuaia towards the sea with hindsight probably wasn't one of his better ideas. The pesos, obtained at such great exertion yesterday, had been to pay for this taxi ride. It was not to be taken for granted that the mighty dollar would be accepted in the butt-end of beyond. What had been taken for granted was that we would be able to get back to the butt-end of beyond after said taxi had deposited us several miles outside of it.

The object that had caused this temporary lunacy was the End of the World Train.

It runs along the restored railway line once used by the in-mates from the Ushuaia Prison and the engines, driven and maintained by a Welshman, look as though they should have an enormous key sticking out of the roof of their cabs.

In the great Celtic Diaspora, the Scots went to Canada, the Irish went to America and the Welsh went to Patagonia.

The railway boasts being the most southerly in the world. This was what had sparked Dad's interest. On a previous expedition into Polar Regions, he had spotted and photographed the most northerly locomotive in the world, on a track that no longer goes anywhere outside Ny Ålesund on Spitsbergen. Now he had decided to hunt down its Antipodean counterpart.

The railway line bears the name 'Ferrocarril Austral Fueguino,' the 'Southern Fuegian Railway,' but one can hardly begrudge its operators bestowing upon it its more romantic pseudonym. After all, it doesn't sound terribly inspiring to say 'I'm going on the First Great Western,' when travelling to Britain's most southerly railway station. There is an Argentine Great Western railway company (British-owned) but I doubt it operates out of London Paddington. Although had he wandered in over the mountains from Peru and got on the wrong train, that may explain how a certain bear ended up there.

The End of the World Station is quite a sizable facility for a station that only runs two scheduled services a day. I've stood on numerous bleak platforms more deserving of the accolade 'End of the World' with any connotations of isolation and apocalypse it may carry. The building is smart and brightly painted and it is only upon raising your eyes from it to look at the mountains behind it towards which the narrow gauge line runs that you realise how utterly bizarre it is, this beautiful, neat little railway station, in the middle of nowhere, its tracks leading to... nowhere, just a few miles into the National Park in which the railway is located and back again..

'I stay a minute,' the taxi driver said as we got out.

Maybe he hoped to get a fare from passengers wanting to return to Ushuaia when the train got back. For the first time I started to feel a little niggle of logistical doubt. We hadn't thought about that. Had we naively assumed there would be a taxi rank at the End of the World Station like at Glasgow Central or King's Cross? (When thinking of dystopic connotations, King's Cross *is* one of those stations deserving of the title 'End of the World.') And ours was the last train of the day. (Or second, depending on how one chose to look at it.) There would be no-one arriving for the next one leaving a conveniently empty taxi standing by the station.

Tomas el Tank Engine was chuffing along a siding, his driver, who I recognised from a book Dad had produced one evening when I was home for Christmas, leaning out of the cab. This is not as facetious as it may sound. One of the engines which operate the line is a 2-6-2 tank imported from the UK. And like his driver, Tomas is Welsh.

Another of the oversized wind-up toys sat beneath an awning that appeared to satisfy the requirements for an engine shed. Percy was obviously taking a siesta.

We left Tomas and his driver to continue their shunting manoeuvres, to which there didn't seem to be an obvious purpose, and went to buy our tickets. The station building housed a bar and peeping through the window I saw a man and a woman in their early twenties, with large rucksacks occupying the spare seats at their table-of-four. Other passengers, obviously. That was encouraging.

'Two please,' Dad said to the station master, who sat in the ticket office behind a plethora of no doubt informative leaflets in a multitude of languages; whether Latin and classical Greek were among them I didn't think to look. I'm pretty sure Gaelic wasn't, but Welsh might have been.

The station master shook his head.

'No, no, sorry. No train.'

Thinking that he might have thought we meant the midday train and had missed it, Dad pulled a printout from the infallible internet from his pocket.

'For this train,' he said pointing to the 1500hrs departure for National Park Station.

'No, no, sorry,' the stationmaster said again. 'Big boat come in Ushuaia. Lots of people. They all on the train.'

'Sold out? No tickets left?'

'They take the train. Only people from the big boat are on the train.'

We looked at each other in puzzlement. Then,

'Chartered,' Dad said, realisation having dawned. 'A cruise ship's chartered the train.'

The taxi driver wouldn't be getting a fare from that then… the taxi! I turned round, bounded to the door and looked out. It was still there, the driver's door open while he stretched his legs out into the sun.

'Sorry,' the stationmaster said again. At least here was one Argentinean who knew how to apologise, even if it wasn't for anything that was his fault.

Dad looked like a little boy denied the train set he had wanted for Christmas. In a way, I suppose that's what he was.

But the stationmaster suddenly remembered something.

'There are two people…' he began, and then as if on cue the young man I had spotted in the bar appeared.

'Is that your taxi?' he asked in a mercifully English voice.

Dad now looked out the door to check that it was still there. There may have been a momentary fear that the young Englishman was about to follow up with, 'Well, it's just gone.'

The driver was back inside now and the door was closed, but the window was wide open and he was leaning back in his seat. He didn't *look* like he was about to drive off.

'Yes.'

'Are you going back to Ushuaia?'

'I suppose we are,' Dad said, his disappointment evident in his voice. 'We can't get on the train.'

The young woman had now arrived and was hovering by her boyfriend's shoulder.

'Can we get a lift back with you?' he asked with such hope that suggested they'd been sitting in that bar for quite a while before we arrived.

'Of course,' Dad instantly brightened, the prospect of helping someone cheering him up.

That, and probably the realisation that that could so easily have been us.

What to do with an unexpected afternoon in Ushuaia.

I wondered what everybody else was doing. The second flight from Buenos Aires would be arriving soon, hopefully with the abandoned suitcases aboard ready to be re-united with their owners. For the first time the question flitted through my mind: what if they didn't turn up?

Strolling along the sea front, a very windy sea front and putting a brave, high-latitude-native face on it we passed a large sign advertising "Transporte Puky Weekend Body." I have no idea what a Puky Weekend Body might be in this context and decided that I would rather not dwell on the possible interpretations, implications or connotations. Perhaps it was the "Transporte" that was "Puky." We were on the edge of the Drake Passage, after all. I prided myself on having not suffered from the effects of "puky" transport for seventeen years (and eight-year-olds are allowed to be seasick, especially after drinking cherry cola).

Lying in the bay was the cruise ship whose passengers had chartered the train. I glowered at her, a convenient scapegoat for our spoiled afternoon. Some Argentine Navy vessels were congregated nearby, keeping a watch on the visitors to their harbour – the white, anonymous cruise ship at anchor in deep water and, tethered to the pier like the stoic pack animal she was, our ship, *Nordnorge*.

Nordnorge first sailed into our lives in April 2001. She appeared in Stornoway Harbour, dwarfing the other vessels, including our lovely 'big' new ferry. She had had a nasty incident involving rocks near Nesna, between Ornes and Sandnessjoen, and was on a short cruise to demonstrate that all repairs were satisfactory.

Dad spotted her from the top of a hill about a mile inland. The road sweeps over the crest, giving a broad panorama of the town and harbour for a brief moment before your car is sucked down into a valley. Even at that distance, and within such a limited window of ocular opportunity the distinctive red band on the ship's hull was clearly visible.

The delight still beams out from him every time he tells the story.

'And I thought, "I know what that is!"'

'That' was the livery of the Hurtigrute. The Norwegian Coastal Express. It has been in operation since 1883, originally between Trondheim and

Hammerfest on the west coast of North Norway, but over the years this has been extended both to the north and south.

Today the ships run north out of Bergen, following each other up the coast to Kirkenes then back south again. The daily departures from Bergen for which the route is particularly well known did not start until 1936, but since then, interrupted only by the Second World War, the ships have continued their perpetual motion up and down the coast, 365 days a year providing a service to the many remote towns and villages only easily accessible by sea. Before the advent of the Hurtigrute, mail had taken weeks to get from central Norway to Hammerfest, the most northerly town in the world, a sort of Ushuaia-in-the-mirror. This was shortened to days, and the 'mail boat' heritage is still very much a part of the Coastal Express, the ships proudly flying their post flag from their sterns. Technology has moved on but the Hurtigrute is essentially unchanged. 'Eleven ships, eleven days,' reads the advertisement, thus each port of call has one northbound and one southbound service each day. In the more remote north, village life revolves around the ships, the docks bustling with people, both adults and children, forklift trucks and occasionally entertainment (or mickey-taking) for the tourists. Then as soon as the ship casts off they all vanish, dissolving into the barely glimpsed village behind, the pier silent until the next ship arrives. Much as it was in my hometown not so long ago that I don't remember the arrival of the ship being the excitement of the day. The irony is poetic, that in a time when cruises are becoming more and more popular (even though many of those who go on them seem to want to pretend that they're not at sea at all) the 'cruise' described as 'The Most Beautiful Voyage in the World' is not a cruise at all, but simply these tough, working ships doing their job.

The Express was originally operated by a single shipping line, but was never intended to be a monopoly and periodically other lines would join, adding their ships to the caravan. But in 2005, eight months after we returned from the Antarctic, the last two lines in operation on the route merged to form a single company. But for now, *Nordnorge* still wore the pale yellow livery of OVDS on her funnel.

My parents had made the voyage in 1976, before I was born; they'd also circumnavigated Iceland on a cargo boat, taking advantage of a subtle ploy by the master to get priority entrance into ports on account of 'passengers.'

It's not terribly surprising that I ended up the way I did.
Between that great rediscovery in Stornoway harbour and this rendezvous in Ushuaia, 6,000 miles and 112 degrees of latitude away, Dad had travelled with the Hurtigrute a further four times. I accompanied him on two of those occasions, the first being his return to Norway 25 years after that voyage he had made with my mother.

There is a photograph he took of her at the Russian border. You weren't allowed to even photograph Russia then, so he stood with his back to it and took the picture with Norway behind. With that photograph he now keeps one of me, taken in more or less the same spot, but this time his back is to Norway and Russia stretches out behind me. Neither of us knew it at the time, but within a few short years, I would even hold a Russian visa. My mother died less than ten years after her photograph was taken there. How the world has changed since then. I often wonder what she would make of it if she suddenly came back.

That first voyage that Dad and I made to Norway's frozen crown was aboard a ship called *Nordkapp*. *Nordkapp* and *Nordnorge* were the only truly identical sisters in the OVDS fleet, and it seemed fitting that *Nordkapp* would be joining her twin in the Antarctic the following southern summer. What adventures they could have together...

We weren't allowed to go aboard yet, our inquisitive noses being turned away from the gangway, obliging the inquisitive rest-of-us to follow, so the question remained: what to do with an afternoon in Ushuaia?

And I still couldn't hear properly.

Nine years previously I had gone on a trip to California with a friend of mine. Of the two days we spent in San Francisco, the first was with friends from Berkley, across the Bay, who showed us their parts of the city. The second, left to our own devices, we... went round exactly the same places again. I didn't want to risk an argument. At the time, it just wasn't worth it.

I didn't get to Lands End in Golden Gate Park. I had wanted to watch the sunset from there. As it was I didn't even get to go there.

I didn't get to see the 49ers play, even though there was a game on and afterwards one of our friends said it would have been easy to get tickets as it was only a pre-season warm-up. I watched it on TV, but I wasn't allowed to watch the post-game analysis.

I didn't get to ride a cable car.

Yeah, I went to San Francisco.

What did you see?

Chinatown.

Twice.

Go to San Francisco to see Chinese stuff. There's a Chinatown in London, for crying out loud.

But it was my failure to visit Alcatraz that now epitomized Wasted Opportunity.

This was very much on my mind as we wandered down the corridor lined with cells.

The prison had become the Museo Maritimo y ex Presidio de Ushuaia. The 'Museo Maritimo' appealed, of course, and I was perhaps a little guilty of 'Canwecanwecanwe?' with regards to visiting it.

Dad had briefly visited it before, but only to enquire as to whether the little steam engine which had once operated the Prison Railway was there. He was told it was not. He didn't ask again.

The museum turned out to be far more 'ex Presidio' than 'Maritimo' but this did allow me to make some sort of vicarious amends for not visiting Alcatraz.

I peeped into each cell as I passed, refusing to miss a thing. Then my eyes gave a yelp of surprise. The man was sitting on a narrow bunk, wearing an overall covered in little black arrows. (Gosh, I thought. They really did wear things like that, and what was the significance?) It was as though I was gazing through a hole in the universe, that on the other side of that door frame it was 1936 and the poor prisoner was sitting so still simply because there was no point in moving. Or that his punishment had not merely been incarceration but to be suspended in time as well and he had just been forgotten about when the prison closed fifteen years later.

Trotting on, I expounded upon my theories, inspired more by a hyperactive imagination and lack of sleep than any sound basis in physics or temporal mechanics, to Dad who either wasn't listening or couldn't hear me – my auditory affliction had made me so paranoid about talking too loudly that I'd gone to the opposite extreme and had been mumbling all afternoon. I didn't notice that for a moment I'd been ambling along not only mumbling nonsense but mumbling nonsense to myself.

Dad's voice from back down the corridor somewhere broke into my diatribe.

'It is!'

I had a pretty good idea what *it* was. The joy in his voice washed away all the earlier disappointments of the day. He hadn't got his train set, but here was the real thing.

He was peering through a window that looked out onto a courtyard formed by the vacant space between two wings of the prison. I reversed – like a shunting human tank engine myself – and stood on my toes, pulling myself up by the tips of my fingers on the ledge to see out.

The little engine that had once operated the prison railway sat unassumingly in that anonymous in-between place on a short stretch of track, looking tired and emaciated, like a mistreated prisoner herself, but still gallantly protecting her one remaining coach.

The little locomotive was waiting patiently for us when we arrived. The courtyard was much the same as numerous other similarly formed courtyards, and with regards to general sense of direction, if water in the southern hemisphere can't find its way down the drain the right way, what hope do any of us have? But we'd found it, and that was all that mattered and for the moment I left Dad to his forensic examination and photography. I would have to borrow Dad's camera to take my shots. Mine was in my case, which (hopefully) was on board the ship by now. I went to investigate a second heap of machinery on a plinth, a steam engine of some description, but, alas, inferior.

'What's that?' Dad called over.

'Not sure,' I replied. 'But it's not self-ambulatory.'

'Self-ambulatory? That's a good word.'

I rather thought it was, and resolved to use it again.

I returned my attention to the locomotive and her solitary coach. She had once had a whole train of coaches. Now there was just one left. The era to which she belonged had gone, but she still had one coach, another survivor from that by-gone time to keep her company.

What was this small machine, this assemblage of moving parts, parts which would never move again? Her history was of no personal significance to either of us. Her job had been the somewhat ignominious one of taking prisoners to their punishment. She may have been part of the administration of justice, but to paraphrase Wilkie Collins, 'Topsey-turvey sympathies' tend to lie with the perpetrators rather than the victims of crime. And to blame the tool rather than the hand that operates it. Was it *Enola Gay*'s fault that the atomic bomb was dropped on Hiroshima? (But I don't like submarines. Submarines are sneaky. *You can't see me, but I can still GET YOU!* U-20, the U-boat which torpedoed *Lusitania, was* complicit in the deed.)

We were delighted to find this little steam engine not because of anything she had done in her working life nor what she had been, but because she *was.*

Dad had been looking for the most southerly steam locomotive in the world simply because she existed. And the delight at finding her was all the greater because he was not certain that she still did.

But how easily she might have had her place usurped by the young upstarts at the End of the World Station. While they may have appeared to fulfil the technical criterion of being the most southerly steam locomotives in the world, they were only there because this ancient, tired little thing had once trundled up and down that track, since re-laid, every day of her working life more than sixty years ago. She was more deserving of the honour than they.

We discovered later on consultation of a map that the Museo Maritimo y ex Presidio de Ushuaia is further south than the End of the World Station.

Something that was a mere imitation that had seemed so perfect, until cruelly denied... and the real thing then offered instead. Is this perhaps what the resurrection that St Paul writes of to the Corinthians is like? Or is it what life itself is like – the imitation is wonderful, bright and shiny and we genuinely want it because we don't believe there is anything else. But then we find the real thing, and old and rusty as it may be it has a beauty that transcends age and the corporeal form and we can't imagine how we could ever have settled for anything else.

Making our way back to the ship we crossed the taxi rank where we had been deposited a few hours ago and taken our leave of the young Englishman and his girlfriend, who had thanked Dad profusely to the last, to which he had said each time, 'Not at all, not at all,' and refused to accept the pesos thrust at him, telling them that we would have been making the journey anyway (either that, or he just didn't want any more of the damn things).

Making the journey anyway. How easily we might not have been. Was some form of divine providence watching over us? Or was it the young couple who were divinely protected, and we were merely the instruments of that protection, saved in order to save? I recalled the brightening of Dad's dejected spirits when he realised he was able to help someone and so spread our own good fortune around. So perhaps should those who have been offered a return from the wilderness be trying to find people to take back in the taxi with them.

But there are many pieces on the chessboard that encompasses the lives of all who walk the earth, or ever have, or ever will, and under the skill of the Grand Master they will interact with each other for mutual good.

Watched over. Permitted to wander, but not cut off. One may go to the wilderness but under some omniscient, omnipotent eye there is always a way back. And a chance to bring others back who've wandered off and got lost.

We arrived at our cabins to find our suitcases waiting for us by the doors, like two dogs who'd run on ahead on the way back from a long walk and were now eager to be let back into the house. Their journey this time had not been too arduous. We had taken them from the bus and deposited them in a marquee on the pier with big labels with our names and cabin numbers on them, a system identical to that operated when boarding a Hurtigrute ship in Bergen, and the ship's porters had brought them on board. But even for that short journey, and even though Norwegians generally command my complete trust, just leaving them there and hoping they would turn up where were supposed to wasn't as easy as it might have been forty-eight hours ago. How easily my bag, which had been everywhere with me since my first trip to Norway, and the contents of Dad's, if not the suitcase itself, might not have been sitting by our cabin doors, but somewhere vanished into the ether between England and Argentina. It had been even odds, fifty-fifty, depending on which flight we had been re-booked onto after the cancellation of ours.

The will of God is incontrovertible. Such is the stoic mantra of the pious sufferer. But I put to you the words of a Job turned around to philosophy happier but no less true:

'Shall we accept ill from God and not good?'[3]

God the Father, who knows how to give good gifts to His children,[viii] intended that Jack Kernahan should find that little engine. Perhaps because in herself she was nothing special, old and weary and sitting in the grounds of a former prison, but because she simply existed he wanted to find her, and his motive was pure enough for the One who had said, 'Seek and ye shall find.'[ix]

But the Grand Master watched the movements of the pieces across the

---

[3] A corruption of Job 3:10

board, and saw the outcome of the play at hand. As so often happens when we make our own plans to achieve our aims, we wander off along the wrong path.

The Grand Master moves His pieces.

If they take a trip on the End of the World Train, they will not visit the museum, they will be stranded miles from the town with a ship to catch and they will not be able to help My two other children who are stranded there.

Our blundering off on our own resulted in the 'rescue' of two stranded backpackers. So was that particular move truly free, or was it engineered by the movements of other pieces? Was Dad really straying from some pre-ordained divine desire that he should find the Prison Train (what remains of it) by following a convincing red herring and trying to get to the End of the World Railway, settling for the counterfeit, sour grapes turned to sweet gooseberries, when the genuine article was, unknown to him, within reach (and a lot nearer and with no logistical risks attached, Shanks' pony being the most suitable means of getting there)? Or was it all part of a recovery operation to get a young couple out of the pickle He knew they were going to get themselves into?

Every move of every piece on a chessboard the size of the universe.

The pawns pick their way across it, preyed upon and vulnerable. But when they reach the other side, they may become whatever they choose. The humble pawn, if it perseveres, can become the most powerful piece on the board.

**

Each Hurtigrute is unique.

Although *Nordnorge* and *Nordkapp* are identical from their exterior and they have identical deck plans, their décor, furnishings and interior lighting are almost entirely different, and of course there is the being of the ship herself. In this way they are not dissimilar to human identical twins. So it was with a sense of nearly-but-not-quite déja-vu that I leaned my forearms on the railing next to Dad in a spot corresponding to the one we had so often occupied on board *Nordkapp* (right at the stern, to starboard of the jack-post, Dad next to it, me to his left). Indeed the similarities in our mannerisms are somewhat akin to those between sister-ships. Later in the voyage a friend we were yet to meet would take a photograph of Dad standing in this spot from 'above and behind' all wrapped up in his cold weather gear. He was adamant that it was me. I was equally adamant that it was him. I pointed out that the green beanie hat belonged to him. And yes – we had all been given identical red expedition-issue jackets, which the pair of us were now trying out. But I still had to remind myself that *Nordnorge* was a new acquaintance.

I'm not my sister.

But I knew that didn't mean we wouldn't get on just as well.

Dad wandered off.

ORION IS UPSIDE DOWN

I returned to my cabin to take inventory of my photographic equipment, among it a prized acquisition – a circular polarizing filter. Almost a day's wages had gone on this small piece of dark glass, but if it delivered it would be worth it. I couldn't wait to try it out, and offered up a prayer of thanks once again that it was neither in Heathrow/Madrid/Buenos Aires/Timbuktu with the contents of eighteen other suitcases or in the possession of a random Argentinean who didn't know how to say 'Sorry.'

I had just finished stowing my kit in my camera bag when my nose started to tickle. I was going to sneeze. This was my chance. A friend of Dad's had ended up in hospital by doing something like this, but I was desperate. I pinched my nose and clamped my eyes shut.

My ears snapped rather than popped (Crackle didn't make an appearance) and boy, did it *hurt*, but Hallelujah! I could hear!

I was all but singing (delighted that I could pitch my voice again) as I detoured to the library on the way to dinner to read the newspaper. The newspapers were literally that – A4 sheets of paper pinned to the wall with the headlines, financial reports and sports results for each country represented on board.

The news from England was not good. My beloved Tottenham Hotspur had lost 3-1 to Southampton, who were heading for relegation from the Premiership that season.

I no longer felt like singing.

The owners of the errant suitcases didn't have anything to sing to about yet either.

Dad had been talking to the crew. The ship was going to wait until midnight, 'And if they've not shown up by then, we're leaving.'

Turned out he knew the courier. We were on a Norwegian ship in Tierra del Fuego about to depart for the Antarctic, and Dad knew the courier. Her name was Karen and she had been on board *Nordnorge* when Dad had made a voyage down the Chilean Fjords and across to the Peninsula two years before. Then they'd bumped into each other again, this time on board *Finnmarken* when that ship had visited Stornoway in 2004. On that occasion he had presented her with a beautiful framed photograph he'd taken of *Finnmarken* in Stornoway Harbour on her previous visit. (The Hurtigrute are no strangers to my wee hometown, as you may have gathered. Other black-and-red-hulled visitors have been *Lyngen,* formerly *Midnatsol II,* an unfortunate vessel beaten with the ugly stick before leaving the shipyard, and *Fram,* the other end of the spectrum of maritime beauty, an adorable ship described as 'a baby *Finnmarken*' who had been commissioned especially for the polar voyages both north and south.)

I love the restaurants on the Hurtigrute. They are right in the stern (typical Norwegian common sense, really, as this is generally the most stable part of the ship) in a manner reminiscent of the magnificent masters' cabins in the sterns of the great ships of sail.

And I always enjoy dinner the first night on board a Hurtigrute. It's a Norwegian institution, the *kalt bord*, a buffet of salad and cold meats and fish. Lots and lots of fish, which suits me fine. If it comes out the sea, chances are I'll like it. Except caviar. The *kalt bord* on board *Nordkapp* four years ago had given me the opportunity to try it. It's revolting. Cod roe is infinitely superior.

I spotted the man who'd been looking for Andreas on the plane, apparently looking for him once again, and Loud Englishman was audible if not visible. Two elderly ladies were sitting by a window, discussing in unmistakably Glaswegian tones how exciting it had all been so far, tempered with concern for the whereabouts of their suitcases. I smiled, and I felt it touch my eyes with a sweet sadness as I remembered my grandmother. My friends used to say that my gran was Supergran.[4] She was in her early nineties when she died, and she lived every minute of it. She would have loved this.

Usually I like to 'watch proceedings' as Dad calls it – hang over the side watching as the ropes come off. Older ships edge away from the dock by means of co-operation between propellers and rudder. The newer ones equipped with bow thrusters, move smoothly sideways through the water. Sometimes I think they're just showing off. But I was exhausted. Going deaf, even temporarily, really takes it out of you. The luggage would have to arrive without me, and I was grateful that I had no vested interest in the outcome.

It was getting dark. I felt an undercurrent of impatience in the deck beneath my feet and in the superstructure surrounding me. *Nordnorge* was eager to be off. The ship's restlessness was not surprising. The Hurtigrute never really stop. They lie at each port a few hours at most, and then it's off again on their continuous voyage up and down the Norwegian coast. No wonder this waiting for suitcases that had had the indecency to get themselves lost was getting to her.

Here I was at the end of the world. What lay beyond? The Drake Passage, reputedly the fiercest of this world's seas, guarding… guarding…my geographical knowledge was melting, as I saw through the eyes and felt with the hearts of those gone before, who had stood on that shore and seen only an unknown Beyond, ignorance and innocence bleeding into one. Then they were gathered souls on the bank of the first of Hell's great rivers.

And Charon took *Nordnorge*'s helm.

Orange glow of the ship's running lights deepening to red, bass-notes of colour seeping through my eyelids. Pulling me down. And I can do nothing but submit.

---

[4] Remember the kids' TV show in the '80s about a Glaswegian granny with superpowers? My gran and my dad both hail from Glasgow. I'm the first wild Highlander for four generations, but that's another story.

They stare out from the confines of their marble, water-less dock, towards the Thames and the greater world beyond – beyond the Estuary, beyond the seas that surround the shores of this Sceptre'd Isle, into the Oceans that encircle the Earth, to places so far away that the waters swallow them, places where even the sky is different. Places ant-artis, *without the Bear, where instead a celestial Ship sails the heavens, her Keel towards the Southern Cross, and where Orion is upside down.*

Their ship is made of dreams and nightmares, all machine and flesh and bone synergised in terrible beauty. And they, fantastical abominations, are wonderful to behold. There is nothing of nature in them yet they are nature.

They are magnificent.

They are terrifying.

They are The Navigators.

The sculpture by David Kemp dominates the atrium of Hayes Galleria on the South Bank in London.

Shackleton set out from here on his final voyage to the Great White South. His ship, Quest, *sailed from Hayes Wharf in October 1921, many old hands aboard her. Frank Wild, the trusty second and Frank Worsley, ship's master who had once performed the greatest feat of navigation in maritime history; surgeons McIlroy and Macklin, and Leonard Hussey, one time persistent would-be navigator, now their assistant, and Charlie Green, the cook. And one Thomas F. MacLeod, able seaman.*

The man who Antarctica could not kill did not return from the Quest *expedition of 1921-22. He died of a heart attack upon the eve of their reaching South Georgia, denying the ice its prey forever.*

He was buried in the Whalers' Cemetery at Grytviken at the insistence of his wife, Emily.

And so he waits, on the edge of that final wilderness with which he battled again and again and again, which could never defeat him, but neither could he defeat it. Now they are poised in eternal stalemate.

His grave faces south.

From out of the space once occupied by Quest, *now filled and paved over with elegant craftsmanship the metal monstrosity leers at me, weak creature of flesh.*

Go.

CHAPTER 3
The Drake Passage

Cape Horn was a legend. It was a place that I had been hearing about all my life in the sea stories I had so loved as a child and continued to love as I grew up. It was a place of shipwrecks; it was a place where Nature was in charge and the insignificance of Man laid bare; it was the place where the great oceans of the world, the Atlantic and the Pacific, raged in endless combat with each other, heedless of the tiny ships and even tinier human beings caught up and tossed around, many times to their deaths, in the cross-fire of their battle. The ocean around Cape Horn was never beaten. It simply allowed those who prevailed to pass. The crew of the *Bounty*, at that time still under the command of Captain Bligh, tried unsuccessfully for four weeks to round the Horn, and in the end chose to sail all the way around the world instead rather than continue to face the wrath of those seas.

The weather conditions which met *Nordnorge* after leaving the shelter of the Magellan Strait made it easy to see why. In twenty-five years of regular passage on the seas off the west coast of Scotland I had never experienced such a rough sea. I would have been disappointed had it been otherwise.

The first thing I was aware of as I awoke was the motion of the ship. I think *Nordnorge* had decided I had been asleep long enough and was trying to throw me out of my bunk.

Come on, get up. We've been out here for ages. You're missing it all!

Just as well she did, because we were approaching the Horn and I had managed to sleep through my alarm.

Showering was like something out of a comedy, *Some Mothers Do 'Ave 'Em*, perhaps, or *Monty Python*. The water kept sloshing out of the cubicle and all over the floor and I'm sure Frank Spencer could have performed some marvellously dangerous feats of acrobatics, even in that tiny toilet area, but I certainly wasn't keen on doing my own stunts. Especially not before breakfast. But after my adventures with the wobbling shower cubicle my balance was shot to pieces – though it would probably been much worse if I hadn't got my ears to pop the previous evening – and when I arrived downstairs I didn't really feel like breakfast.

Dad brought me a cup of tea.

We forced our way out on deck against winds stronger than anything I'd encountered at sea, or on land, before. The sky was a field of grey, levitating above a stampeding herd of white horses that surrounded the ship as far as the horizon, unbroken save for one dark land mass off the starboard bow – the Horn.

The ship creaked and groaned in a manner more associated with tortured timbers in the age of sail than a modern steel ship. I stood beneath a lifeboat, imagining that it afforded some shelter, struck with awe by the spectacle taking place before me. Nothing prepares you for this. *Mad as the sea and wind*, said Shakespeare's Gertrude of her son, *when both contend which is the mightier?* I had no answer. These wild horses had raced here since the continents took up their present positions, regardless of whether a boatload of humans was watching or not, before there even were humans to watch. Nature does not dance for our entertainment. On occasions we may be privileged enough to be permitted to observe, but we are peeping in from outside, not sitting in the stalls. I peered up at the ship's superstructure. The creaking was coming from the davit holding the lifeboat over my head. I moved to the rail, not because I feared the lifeboat would fall, but because I realised it was not offering any shelter worth mentioning. I pulled myself out my pocket of wonder. I *was* in an amazing place, and had had my first exposure as to just how amazing.

Angling my own camera slightly downwards didn't help much in keeping the lens dry. Water hung suspended in the air and mingled with the spray thrown up by the angry sea in vortices of cold wetness that defied gravity. The waters divided on the second day of Creation were trying to recombine here in this wild place, beyond the natural reach of Man.

Staggering slightly as the ship fell away beneath my feet upon her descent from the peak of each wave, I moved right to the stern and planted myself next to the naked jack post where Dad and I had stood the previous evening when we were still tied up at the pier at Ushuaia. I planted my feet wide apart and braced my elbows on the railing, holding the video camera to my face with both hands.

'You have no idea how difficult it is to remain standing!' I bellowed at the microphone.

When I played the film back later my voice was barely audible above the roar of the elements.

With the Cape now disappearing into the heavy weather astern we forced our way back indoors. There was to be a briefing on tomorrow's landing at Deception Island held in the bar, about as far forward in the ship as you can get without going out onto the forecastle. This area was taking the full upward force of every wave the ship rode. Chairs and tables –heavy chairs and tables, intended as furnishings for ocean-going ships – were moving.

'I don't like this,' Dad said.

'It'll be OK,' I replied. 'We can just sit near the back.'

'No, go to your cabin.'

I obeyed.

I returned to my cabin, put everything on the floor and, remembering *Nordnorge*'s treatment of me earlier that morning, lay down there myself to wait it out.

Knock-knock-knock.

'Housekeeping.'

'Could you come back later please?'

I knew she hadn't heard me.

'Housekeeping.'

A little louder, 'No, thank you.'

The door opened and a delicate Filipino face appeared around it.

'Clean your cabin?'

'Leave me alone!'

I was experiencing something unfamiliar and rather unpleasant. I was now curled up on my bunk like a frightened little animal that didn't know what was happening to it. For the first time in seventeen years (and second time in my life) I was seasick.

I went down for dinner ravenous, as I had slept through lunch, and probably wouldn't have wanted any anyway. I soothed my wounded pride by reminding myself that Nelson got seasick the first day out of port. It is just the ocean's way of reminding us who's boss

I wasn't the only one to suffer injury in the Drake Passage, and I can be thankful that mine was only to my dignity. Given the enthusiastic movement of the ship this should perhaps not come as a surprise (Dad has sent me to my cabin for a reason) but 'one hand for the ship' is so much second nature to me (or maybe it would be more truthful to say it was my first nature, really) that the idea that someone didn't think to hold on was somewhat alien. The woman had taken quite a blow to her ribs, it appeared, giving the ship's doctor something to treat other than seasickness. From then on warning signs appeared telling people to be careful and use handrails. Can't imagine that ever happening in Norway, either the injury or the warnings. Norwegians are sensible and tend to assume that other people are as well.

'What happened about the cases?' I asked, trying not to down my Coke in one long slug. As well as being stupidly hungry I had a raging thirst. I wondered if this was a normal part of the aftermath of seasickness.

'Oh, now that's something else you missed,' Dad replied.

I think he was still surprised that I had slept through take-off on the plane to Buenos Aires and had voluntarily gone to bed before the ropes came off. (I was one of those children who just *refused* to go to bed.)

Dad went on to tell of how the shop (singular) in Ushuaia had been persuaded to open at ten o'clock last night (ten o'clock? Was I asleep by ten o'clock?) to allow the unfortunate owners of the suitcases to replace the essential items that were now somewhere other than Ushuaia, receipts carefully stowed away for presentation to a certain Spanish airline upon return. Bet they weren't expecting *that* when they decided to save a few Euros in fuel costs by leaving the bags behind. I could picture a sleek airline manager shrugging in a continental way and saying in a strong Spanish accent, 'We will send the bags on and we will pay compensation. It will not be a problem – whatever their destination, we surely fly there.' And that compensation would, under normal circumstances, be considerably less than the saving in fuel costs. Of course, money soothes all grievances, doesn't it? But it's the airline's focus on the stuff that's caused the situation in the first place. Then the manager is told where the owners of the suitcases are going. There are still places on this earth that are beyond the reach of your mighty airline, Snr Manager. And there are still things on which you cannot place a monitory value.

There's a moral in there.

As Dad was finishing the tale of the nocturnal shopping expedition we were joined by the couple who would be sharing our table. They introduced themselves as Pete and Becky, a retired American couple originally from Washington but now living in the South.

They-With-A-Capital-T, who say Venus is upside down, also say that everyone has a doppelgänger somewhere in the world. Becky was the double of one of my former English teachers. This disturbed me. Even more so when I learned that Pete and Becky had both been teachers. But my former English teacher was Canadian.

They were well travelled and were undoubtedly very intelligent people. So it came as a surprise to me when Pete expressed his view that within the United Nations each state in the USA ought to have a vote because each country in Europe had one.

I wasn't about to start an international incident. By that reasoning, the UK ought to have four votes. Although I was pretty sure that the same geo-political arrogance that had formed Pete's opinion would probably insist that Scotland and England are the same country, would never have heard of Wales, and Northern Ireland... now, there's a powder keg. Literally. Well, five kilograms of Semtex at the time.

But the conversation had moved on and Dad was enjoying telling our companions that the university I had attended (he went there too, but he didn't mention that) was older than their country.

The desserts arrived. Chocolate mousse with vanilla fluffy stuff on top in tall glasses. I'd been so hungry before that I was definitely up for dessert, but all I could do was skim the vanilla off the top and make sure I enjoyed each spoon-tip-full.

'You don't like chocolate?' Becky asked.

I like chocolate a lot (chilli chocolate is one of the greatest inventions by confectioners ever) but I had given it up for Lent. I explained as much, and gave my vanilla-less mousse to Dad.

It was only later that evening, sitting by a window in the corridor lounge on Deck 4 after finding some particularly good oat cookies on offer that compensated for my missing out on the chocolate mousse, that I was able to think about those who'd gone before. Out on deck as we rounded the Horn, all my efforts had been concentrated on staying upright. I find myself in good company. Shackleton had been round the Horn five times by the time he was twenty, on one occasion the ship, a square-rigger called *Houghton Tower*, being held for two months in the warring seas. Her crew were obviously more persistent than that of *Bounty*.

Shackleton was a seaman through and through. At the age of 24 he gained his Master's certificate and so was qualified to command any British ship anywhere in the world. Bored at school, and a perpetual dreamer, he had set his heart on the sea, much to his father's disappointment, who had hoped that his son would follow him into the medical profession. Young Ernest thought that perhaps his father had tried to put him off the idea by 'letting [him] go in the most primitive manner possible.' If that were the case, Dr Shackleton's plan failed. The baptism of fire, or very high water, that Ernest was to undergo aboard *Houghton Tower* would stand him in good stead several years later when he would join one R. F. Scott aboard *Discovery*.

I was most impressed by *Discovery* when I first visited her some eighteen months before my journey south, with her propeller and rudder assembly that can be hoisted out of the water to prevent damage from ice, and her iron-clad stem, plates of armour over her wooden prow; she is an icebreaker.

I am a little in awe of ice-breakers. Ships designed to break the ice, which usually does its damnedest to break *them*. They're strong. They're tough. They're heroic. I had tended to think of them as a product of modern technology, but here I was in the presence of one of the earliest. Her weaponry is offensive – those iron plates enable her to cut through the ice – but wood withstands better than steel the pressure exerted by the ice when it takes a ship in its grasp. Her structure is designed for defence. It seems somehow fitting that in a land beyond time that which is perceived as being weak when compared to the advances of modern technology should be stronger. The meek shall inherit the earth. It makes sense that in the Antarctic a more 'primitive' vessel should be better suited to it. Biologists will tell us that the most primitive organisms are the most resilient. Lichens. Mosses. Penguins are considered to be such a primitive species of bird that at the time of Scott's fateful *Terra Nova* expedition in 1910 it was believed that they could offer a valuable insight into the evolution of reptiles into birds, so much so that Apsley Cherry-Garrard and his companions set off on 'the worst journey in the world' in order to obtain some eggs. These are the natives of Antarctica, not humans. *Discovery* is a point of evolution as maritime engineering made the awkward transition from sail to steam, from wood to steel, but it was her less advanced qualities that made her so well suited to her environment.

So. You've been.

Yes.

It is three months since my return from the Antarctic. As on my previous visit, the presence of Shackleton is far more prevalent than that of Scott.

The ship makes no reply, but pulls me toward the wardroom. I have not yet been there this time. For the last few minutes I have been standing beneath her bell.

The bell is the soul of a ship. If a ship is lost, maritime tradition insists that her bell, if at all possible, must be recovered. It is the symbolic raising of the ship. But as ships have ceased to be 'shes' and have become 'its' other traditions have also fallen away.

The main accommodation area on ships such as Discovery, *and* Shackleton's Endurance *too, is beautifully simple. The wardroom, where meals were taken, discussions held and plans made is flanked by cabins, so everybody lives side by side with their tiny private worlds opening onto the communal area. There is no shipboard real-estate distinction between the officers (the seamen lived and slept below, some are always more equal than others) and Captain Scott's cabin differs from that of, say, Reginald Skelton, only in the personal effects it contains.*

I step up to the velvet-covered cordon that ropes off his cabin.

I went to the cemetery.

I know. It's in your heartbeat.

Another silence. Her scent fills my nostrils. There's nothing like the essence of a ship. It's not a smell as such, but it enters through the olfactory nerves.

I think he'd like it if you went in.

I don't reply. He's walked these decks, stood beneath these masts, climbed that rigging, isn't that enough?

You travelled six thousand miles to stand by his grave. I think he'd like it if you sat on his bunk.

I approach the curator.

'Hi,' I say, but the voice hardly seems like mine. 'I know this is asking a lot...'

The curator nods and smiles and unfastens the velvet rope. I go in. She returns to the other side of the wardroom, leaving me alone. Discovery *herself retreats a little as well.*

I sit down on the lower bunk.

'Boss, there's something I forgot to say...'

***

The verse in Revelation 'And there was no more sea'[x] when John described the New Heaven and the New Earth had always troubled me. How Heaven could be, well, Heaven without sea was incomprehensible to me. If there was no sea in Heaven, did I really want to go there? What did that make me? A rebel soul? Was that sufficient to damn me? Was that perhaps how Satan won souls to his domain, not by convincing them that his way was better, but that by making them believe that eternity with the Ancient of Days might not be all it's cracked up to be.

But then, what of the alternative? Ice at the very centre of Hell. And not a landscape of ice, but a seascape, a frozen lake, the frozen lake Cocytus. Marine ice, that which struck terror into my soul.

Lucifer may have made his declaration 'Better to rule in Hell than serve in Heaven,'[xi] but I firmly believe that it would be far preferable to spend eternity without the ocean than be bound endlessly in ice.

Why should there be 'no more sea' in Heaven when the oceans were part of creation, that on the third day of Creation, the Lord gathered together the waters under heaven such that dry land appeared, and the waters He called Sea. And, as with the rest of Creation, 'the Lord saw that it was good.'[xii]

Heaven may not necessarily be landlocked after all. The language of Revelation is highly symbolic, no-one surely would argue with that. Who would sensibly understand images of beasts with excessive numbers of heads and horns as literal, even in the strictest Fundamentalist circles? Revelation, like it would often seem, the rest of the Bible, is only taken literally when our twenty-first century vision permits it. The rest becomes conveniently metaphorical.

The Hebrew word for 'sea,' *yam,* is the same as the word for 'chaos.'

'And the Spirit of God moved upon the face of the waters.'[xiii] And the Spirit of God descended upon the chaos, when all was void and without form. I'd always held in my mind the image of the Spirit of God as an immense pair of wings. I am unable to see what manner of being is held aloft by these wings because I am looking out from within it. But I see the wings spread out over a vast and wild ocean, untamed, untempered, unfettered by the presence of land, covering the whole globe of the earth. And He moved upon it and calmed it and set its boundaries. Beautiful and awesome as this concept may be, it is nothing more than a metaphor conveying a truth, simple but humanly incomprehensible in any other form, my vision nothing more than my imagination and intellect working together to allow me to process that truth – that God made order out of chaos.

The sea as chaos?

Where does that leave me, having just escaped from dissatisfaction at the geography of the New Heaven and the New Earth I now find myself loving chaos. Loving something civilised humanity balks at. Loving something so contrary to the will of God that His Spirit descended to impose that will upon it.

But far from being chaotic, the ocean carries some of the most fundamental rhythms in nature. The tides, currents, the Great Ocean Conveyor. Perhaps that then is God imposing His will – what once was wild and uncontrolled has been made a slave, a slave to the moon, the sun, global temperatures. As the Archangel Michael will one day bind Lucifer in chains, so in the act of Creation did God put chains upon the sea. Upon Chaos.

He set its boundaries. But that doesn't stop it grinding them away. Like Jacob wrestling the angel, the sea strives against the limits imposed upon it. Nature wrestling with God's will.

Is this too the result of the Fall? Had there been no Fall, would the sea rage so and hammer at the cliffs and erode and wash away or would it be placid, a true Pacific Ocean, with no waves or tides or movement? Rebellious thoughts surface once again. Wouldn't that be *boring*?

The sea is primal. It appears as the Before in the creation mythology of many ancient cultures. In the void between creations Vishnu sleeps cradled in the coils of an enormous snake floating on a vast ocean. The Egyptian primordial mound emerged from Nun, a boundless watery abyss that existed before the gods. The Greeks, who gave us the word 'chaos,' applied it to the amorphous mass of nothing that was all that existed before the beginning of time, encircled by an endless river ruled over by Oceanus.

But between all these myths and the Hebrew creation story there is one vital difference. In each of the others the primordial ocean exists before creation. Only in the Hebrew account is the primordial ocean created by the Creator. For the Hebrew begins, 'In the beginning God created the heaven and the earth... and the Spirit of God moved upon the face of the waters.' The other creation myths are of how the gods made order out of chaos. Only in the Hebrew does the Creator create the chaos. Since the foundation of Judeo-Christianity is that God, Yahweh, is good, He cannot have created evil. Evil is not a created thing but a state arising from the misuse of Free Will. And since God created chaos, the untamed ocean, it cannot be evil.

The salinity of human protoplasm is the same as that of the primordial sea from which life is believed to have arisen.

The grinding away of rocks, the lashings against the cliff faces, straining at the chains, beating at the boundaries set for it during the act of Creation, the howling desire of nature to rebel against the will of God and return to chaos cannot be evil. It is primal, ancient beyond our comprehension.

When the ocean defies all which tries to keep it bound in the relentless rhythm imposed upon it, it is easy to see why these ancient civilisations associated the sea with chaos.

The storm.

The fury of the caged beast raging to be free.

Straining to return to chaos.

I love the ocean, chaos and all. It is a part of what it is.

The ocean is worth the storm.

CHAPTER 4
The Peninsula

At 2am, almost sixteen hours after leaving the tail of South America behind, we crossed the Antarctic Convergence, where the Atlantic and Pacific Oceans whose perpetual warfare we had been caught up in meet, although how such a point of rendezvous can be accurately ascertained I have no idea, and thus entered Antarctic territory. Thankfully *Nordnorge* didn't try to wake me for the occasion. The ship now flew no courtesy flag.[5] These waters belong to no one. Or to everyone.

With no indigenous human population, this is the last expanse of Creation as God intended it, untouched by fallen humankind. Is this perhaps why we have always known it to be there, even although there was no ocular proof until a couple of hundred years ago, and even then it was mostly shadowy sightings and sailors' tales? Is this what remains of Eden?

In the early afternoon the first icebergs appeared off the port bow. Two rogue bergs, separated from the pack. Forward sentinels of the silent army guarding the approaches to the frozen continent, this Eden guarded not by a flaming sword but by moving mountains of ice.

Of course we are 'encroaching' on Antarctica. There is a human presence, there are emissions from their technology, there is a hole in the ozone layer. I'm not talking about a pristine wilderness as Eden. I'm talking about something more fundamental. I said, 'no *indigenous* human population.' No branch of the human family tree evolved there, no dust of the Antarctic continent was formed into a man into whose nostrils was breathed life.

Antarctica is untied to humanity. If Creation fell with man, Antarctica has no part in that. Antarctica is unfallen. Antarctica is sinless.

I was happy that my sea-legs were asserting themselves. I had been concerned that they wouldn't – this was the longest time I had been at sea with no landfall – and that I would spend the voyage staggering around like some ungainly land animal who had no right to be there. The pitching of the ship had not lessened since our encounter with Cape Horn, but I was relieved to find that it was not causing me any real problems with locomotion.

Until I tried to run.

I had quite fancied the idea of jogging round and round the deck, like they do in old war films, getting cold and wet from the spray but soldiering on because I'm *hard*. But the ship and the elements had other ideas. Gone were the dark clouds and damp mists of the Cape and the sun was shining down upon us from the north (which was still confusing me) but as I approached the bow, being forced to accelerate as *Nordnorge* dipped her head over the top of a swell, the wind whipped me, sending me skidding into the railing. There was no risk of me tumbling over – I'm so short that the top of the rail is just above mid-chest height – but I had no desire to slide all over the deck every time had to come round that corner. Also the ship's pitching, while not a complete show-stopper, was annoying.

So, no brave, 'I'm-not-going-to-let-being-at-sea-in-the-middle-of-the-Southern-Ocean-stop-me' running round the deck then.

I would have to find an alternative.

---

[5] A foreign ship flies at her mast the flag of the country in whose waters she is sailing.

Find a way, or make a way.[6]

I was training for my first marathon, and sixteen days with no exercise would not have been conducive. Paula Radcliffe's autobiography had become something of a second bible to me as I sought encouragement. The image of her sitting on the kerb having dropped out of the Marathon at the Athens Olympics both haunts and inspires me. Paula is another whom I admire as much for their failures and how they have overcome them as for their successes. The storm rages, the rumbling thunder of defeat comes closer and closer and the rain of failure lashes down and washes away the clay feet of the idol. It topples and smashes, revealing the vulnerable human being inside. It is those who stand up shake off the debris and face the storm who are the true heroes, not those who are found cowering inside the wreckage of the golden shell. And should that storm never come, should that shell never shatter, the occupant remains hidden by it... or hiding within it. How we deal with failure is a far greater measure of our strength than all the successes we may accumulate.

Radcliffe's grandfather had worked at Grytviken. For all my recent introductions to its vastness, it's often quite a small world.

I stood at the bottom of the stairwell, looking up. The stairs ran almost the entire height of the ship. I quietly considered it idleness for any able-bodied persons to use the lifts, but an awful lot of them appeared to do so. Of course, the term 'able-bodied' is becoming relative and seems to have come to mean 'willing-bodied,' and most of those who think they 'can't' in reality 'won't.' But it would be an unacceptable breach of political correctness to suggest that they 'can' and an even worse one to point out that the reason they have so much difficulty is because... It would probably have done the lift-riders a world of good if they had used the stairs instead. Although having said that, Dad had passed comment that since his last voyage he no longer felt the urge to wander around singing 'Wide, wide as the ocean.' Perhaps that was because a medical examination had been required for this voyage, which had not been previously. I wondered if there had been some sort of incident.

It was the use of the stairwell as a form of physical exercise that I was currently investigating. I tanked it up the stairs. *Nordnorge* is about as tall as a Hurtigrute can be. Their height is limited by the ubiquitous bridges to be found on the Norwegian coast, much as the *QM2*'s was limited by the height of Verranzo Bridge. They didn't consider the Panama Canal when it came to her length and beam though. If the *QM2* is ever to sail around the world, she must go round Cape Horn.

A reasonable effort was required to charge to the top of *Nordnorge*'s stairwell. I got some funny looks from the few stair-climbers I had hurtled past

---

[6] Attributed to Frank Hurley in Channel 4's *Shackleton.* Whether he actually said it or not doesn't really matter. It's a pretty good attitude to have.

on the way up as they saw me coming straight back down again. But it would do.

The evening of a day spent entirely at sea approached, bringing with it that spectrum of colour released by a sun pressed down towards the horizon that must surely come from the pot of gold at the end of the rainbow. It was by this light that we caught our first glimpse of Antarctica, with the appearance of string of islands that nestles alongside the peninsula, as though seeking its protection from the raging oceans. And Antarctica, infamous for her utter hostility to life, shows, on occasions, a quite incongruous tenderness and offers a safe haven from the onslaughts she is so capable of unleashing, almost as though she doesn't *want* to harm anyone and so has provided a safe place for those caught up in the maelstrom to take refuge when she becomes angry. We sailed through the wonderfully named Neptune's Bellows, the only entrance to one such place of safety, and anchored surrounded by the pennanular cliffs of Deception Island.

Deception Island is the flooded cone of an active volcano and it provides a natural harbour that must have seemed a godsend to seamen tossed around on these pitiless waters. But even so, Antarctica doesn't provide that shelter easily. Neptune's Bellows is so named because of the force of the winds that rush through it making navigating the passage difficult and dangerous. But she rewards mariners when they prove themselves worthy and pass through the narrow gap where the turbulent air torments the sea and into the calm beyond.

As an aeronautical engineer I understand the theory behind the behaviour of the elements surrounding Neptune's Bellows. Neptune's Bellows is exactly the same as the working section of a wind tunnel, the air accelerating to pass through a smaller cross-sectional area. But when looking upon, and being buffeted by, Nature in its rawest form doing exactly what we do in our hi-tech laboratories, and think ourselves so clever and 'advanced,' all the equations governing aerodynamics, which Mankind has taken centuries to formulate yet still cannot be fully solved, dissolve to nothing. God is the greatest mathematician of all.

Deception Island was used by sealers in the early 19th century, and later by whalers, first operating factory ships anchored in Whalers' Bay where we were now then from a shore station established in 1912. From the deck I peered out towards the shore trying to see the remains of the station which I knew were still there. The ruins, a mass of corroded iron, merged with the mountains behind as though this human blight long since abandoned was camouflaging itself, hiding from those who had created it. The low sun's strong light touched the rusty oil tanks with the same soft tendrils that caressed the natural rock-face, gilding them, sanctifying them, nature and artifice becoming one. After all, rust is natural. Rust is what happens when iron, that emblem of industry, is returned to the elements. And eventually even the cliffs that now surrounded us, shielding us from much of the onslaught of the ocean would crumble out of sight, eroded away and claimed by the sea. The sea claims all.

'How d'you put this thing on?'

The lifejackets consisted of a halter, which would inflate on contact with water, and a multitude of clips and straps by which it was attached to its wearer, and was more sophisticated and a lot less cumbersome than the permanently buoyant models I was used to. Whoever had worn it last had somehow removed it without undoing the front clip.

Dad turned me around and yanked the straps under my arms. The lifejacket settled snugly against my chest. Then he pulled my hood out from where it was trapped under the halter.

About quarter of an hour ago had begun the logistical masterpiece of getting 270 people ashore without the convenience of a pier. Exit was to be through the car deck, which had been converted into a cross between a water-sports centre locker room and a decontamination unit. Around the walls hung the lifejackets, with a few rogue wetsuits nestled in amongst them, interspersed with racks of Wellington boots with port-and-starboard colour-coding, a blob of red paint on the heel for left and green for right. They had their sizes emblazoned on them as well, but as the sizes were European and Americans and Brits made up more than half the passenger manifest a good deal of empirical experimentation was required. Human traffic was controlled by dividing the ship's compliment into groups of about thirty and calling the next group just as the one currently There were, inevitably, bottle-necks, with some unable to tell their left from their right, and the port and starboard wellies not helping much, but, kitted out in lifejackets, boots and identical expedition-issue red parkas we formed an orderly queue and shuffled like Lemmings (remember the little creatures with green hair and blue overalls from the old Amiga computer game?) through a trough of disinfectant towards an external opening in the hull beyond which was... nothing. I peered out at an aluminium stairway hanging suspended in space several feet above the surface of the water where a fleet of *Polar Cirkle* boats (larger versions of the more familiar Zodiac inflatables) were zipping around, enjoying their freedom after being cooped up for several days and proudly waving little Norwegian flags off their sterns. A couple of those already loaded were whizzing off in the direction of the whaling station. One of the boats was just coasting up to the end of the stairway to nowhere and as she rose and fell on the swell her nose would come level with the end of the stairway twice each oscillation. Two of the ship's crew were doing their best to hold it there, but boarding the boat was like a moving-platform arcade game; missing the platform here would mean a dunking in Antarctic water, though I wondered briefly what effect the active volcano had on the sea temperature. Taking hold of the pilot's arm in a comfortable sailors' grip I dropped into the boat as it was on its way down. It was larger than the Zodiac boats I was used to, and I didn't feel the same urge to lean forward as the boat picked up speed and shot off after those already gone. Our Argentinean guide, Tomas, who had gone ashore ahead, met us at the landing site and took hold of one of the ropes on the boat's prow holding her nose against the shore while her stern continued to bob with the waves.

'Welcome to Deception Island,' he called out and assisted each of us as we plopped off the little boat's bow into ankle-deep water. We had landed on a rocky beach. Where it was visible, the sand was of course volcanic, black, as though the island were in mourning for the acts committed there in what we might consider less enlightened times. As we approached the abandoned whaling station, emerging like something from another world out of the twilight, a few of its current inhabitants regarded us curiously for a moment, but none seemed particularly interested. The seals preferred to go to sleep, probably dismissing us as some species of large red penguin. One of the 'attractions' offered by Antarctic tour operators when visiting Deception Island is the opportunity to swim in the Antarctic. A pit is dug on the beach which fills with ground water warmed by the volcano, Antarctica offering further welcome to her visitors; first a sheltered bay, now hot water. But the baggage debacle had left us several hours behind schedule and the seas had been such that not even a vessel as hardy as *Nordnorge* could make up the time. The twilight that was descending even as we walked along the black beach meant that there would be no swimming here today. At first I was disappointed. *But you don't want that. Come and see what I have to show you.* The station is a crumbling monument to an era now ended, which, however shameful it may now be perceived to be is a part of our human history. To ignore it in favour of splashing about in a hot pool seemed suddenly disrespectful and ignorant. Silly tourists seeking novelty. This was Life, not despite the desolation but because of it, Antarctic 'natives' making it their own after the intruders had moved on. People had lived here, worked here, because they were 'no damn good anywhere else.'[7] It was too dark to take photographs. I was there not as a tourist or as a photographer, but as a human being.

It was definitely getting dark. We were walking along listening to a woman who could best be described as 'spherical,' identifiable as German by her accent and as an Expedition Guide by her yellow parka, talking about penguins – Deception Island is home to the largest chinstrap penguin colony in the world with 100,000 breeding pairs, though most of them must have been asleep – when she was interrupted by a muffled crackling sound coming from her pocket. With an apology she pulled out a walkie-talkie which had been hiding

---

[7] A line from Channel 4's *Shackleton.* A Norwegian whaler at Grytviken is asked why he has chosen such a life. Again, I don't know if anyone ever really said it, but as I've said before, the rest of the film is so accurate that it is entirely possible.

in there and took a few paces away from us to answer the call. It seems a universal truth that any human speech delivered by a walkie-talkie will be incomprehensible to ears more than about two centimetres from the speaker, but I did catch...

'Fffff....worse....fffff....Back to ....ffff .... Ship.'

Our penguin guru finished the discussion with an affirmative – it also seems to be a universal truth that people will nod their heads to express this, even when the person they are talking to can't see them – and turned back to us, walkie-talkie still in her gloved hand.

'The weather is getting bad,' she said. 'We all have to go back to the ship.'

Not everyone had even got to go ashore. Out in the bay I saw one Polar Cirkle boat slowing while its pilot received the message, then turn in a wide circle and go back again. We'd been fortunate to see even this slightly anti-climactic twilight.

Leaving us to return to the waterline where more Polar Cirkle boats were congregating to take us home, she trotted unexpectedly nimbly after a group a little way ahead of us to deliver the news to them. Two other yellow-jacketed guides were also now rounding up people, roles defined, the leaders and the led, identity removed and reduced to the colour of their jacket.

The water was really quite choppy as the boat we boarded sped back to the ship. The stairway clung to *Nordnorge*'s flank, a passageway hanging in the void. The moving platform arcade game had advanced a level. But the sea was now in such a state that missing the platform would probably mean Game Over. The instinctive response was to try to jump up from the boat onto the gangway, and the chap in front of me got himself in a bit of a twist and ended up being hauled unceremoniously onto the platform by a sailor. But you're best stepping down, even though there is something frightening about the prow of the little boat rising above the level of the gangway. Grasping the sailor's arm and stepping off onto the (relatively) stable gangway, I felt quietly chuffed that I did not make the fool of myself that I suspected the man in front expected me to. He'd looked round at me with a look that said, 'If I had trouble, this kid's going in the drink.' Never underestimate little blonde girls, even ones with very short legs. All those hours playing silly computer games had finally paid off.

Deception Island certainly deserves its name. It appears to offer a sheltered haven, but as we had just seen, the waters within its protective ring could rouse themselves as ferociously as any open sea. Yes, it was, by all deceptive appearances, a place of refuge from fierce, high-latitude weather, but it was not necessarily *safe.*

Almost two years later...

Nordkapp ran aground.

It happened while she was leaving Deception Island just as we were now.

Tough, stubborn and self-sufficient, she re-floated herself, but limped back to anchor in Whalers' Bay, listing slightly, awaiting a response to her distress signal.

Nordnorge was northbound, at Port Lockroy, at the time, eight hours away.

Hold on, little sister, I'm coming.

This time the passage through Neptune's Bellows took several hours according to one of those on board. But there to meet her, keeping watch over the wounded, was the namesake of an Antarctic legend.

HMS *Endurance.*

The Royal Navy's Antarctic guard dog.

Icebreaker.

You'll take care of her?

Passengers and luggage were transferred from one Hurtigrute to the other. No-one had been hurt in the incident.

Of course.

Endurance's crew had offered to escort *Nordkapp* across the Drake Passage to safety in Ushuaia.

Nordnorge to *Nordkapp: If you're not careful they won't let you come back.*

Nordkapp to *Nordnorge: They let* you *come back…*

Deception Island behind us, *Nordnorge* charged on into the night, each dip of her head into the on-coming waves throwing up a shower of luminescent spray. On her forecastle, quiet and unassuming, drawing no attention to itself, lay a massive black anchor, bathed in icy brine while its working counterparts nestled inside the ship's bows, port and starboard, chained to their winches.

Its time would come.

Interlude

Had I lost my way?
She is sitting upright on the edge of a great chasm in the sea floor. All geological formations in the ocean make a mockery of their surface counterparts and Titanic's *canyon is no exception. They say she has the best view on Earth to contemplate for eternity. If there was any light down there.*
But is she really the one who is alone in the dark?

I awoke to find myself in a dark wood,
Where the right road was wholly lost and gone…[xiv]

There is *a sea in heaven, before the throne of God, where the redeemed will gather when they have overcome the evils of this world, when they have overcome the beast.*[xv]

The shell perched on the edge of that undersea canyon will crumble and become one with the ocean floor, but she is in the very presence of God.

A friend of mine who is not Fortune's friend
Is hard beset upon the shadowy coast…

But thou, go thou, lift up thy voice of gold;
Try every needful means to find and reach
And free him, that my heart may rest consoled[xvi]

Who paces that shoreline? One perhaps with whom she shares an executioner. He was here to greet her, his frozen shell swallowed by icy oblivion earlier in the year of her own death. Or someone else, who overcame the beast, the beast from out the sea. His shell faces south, ready to do battle once again when the last trumpet blows.

He has served her before, appearing as an expert witness at the inquiry into her loss. He had no agenda, was protecting no-one, simply presenting the truth as he understood it as an authority on ice navigation.

Who better for her to send?

A knight in windproof Burberry…

CHAPTER 5
The Mainland

We were surrounded by giants. Nootaikok, the Inuit god of icebergs, and his court. Tradition describes him as 'large and very friendly.' I wondered which space-time continuum that was in. Certainly not this one. I had mourned the results of his handiwork since I was six years old. *Nordnorge* lay motionless, like one prepared for martyrdom, unarmed before the executioner, yet daring to bring her petition to a god not renowned for mercy, whatever tradition might say.

Of course, the couple of hours of outward inactivity were taken up with the crew's preparations for landing, out of sight down in the car deck, but standing out on deck beneath the lifeboat that had offered so little shelter as we rounded Cape Horn, in the stillness that seemed to be as much a part of the place as the mountains and the water were, it was easy to imagine that the ship was holding parley with the god of the ice, bargaining for the safety of her passengers. Nootaikok acquiesced and the landing began, but the little boats, that the previous evening had gambolled around like puppies, seemed subdued.

They waited patiently for their charges under the lee of *Nordnorge*'s hull, huddling in to the mother-ship for protection.

Be careful, she warned them. *If your propellers hit the ice…*

Ice littered the bay. As well as the bergs, many of them level with the ship's superstructure, the water teemed with brash ice, up to three feet exposed, and the comically named 'bergy bits' that filled the taxonomic gap between brash and true bergs, anything over fifteen feet. And then there were the infamous growlers, barely visible submerged ice that lurked just beneath the surface, like the submarines of some hostile alien power.

The ice here is glacial, ancient. I have heard people say of *Titanic*, 'How could crashing into ice sink a ship?' No one would doubt that crashing into a rock could sink a ship. Glacial ice, the stuff icebergs are made of, is harder than rock. It is not frozen water, it is compressed snow, the ice at and below the surface the oldest, the hardest, compressed over aeons by the mass of hundreds of feet of snow-becoming-ice above it as it makes its slow, unrelenting journey to the sea, gouging its path out of the rock, tearing away the surface as though it were topsoil. Anyone who doubts its destructive power need only look at the fjords of Norway, their sheer cliffs dropping to the sea – ice did that. Destruction that creates.

Tomas helped us ashore again, but he didn't need to hold the Polar Cirkle boat's nose quite as firmly as he had at Deception Island; she was making no attempt to bolt.

'Welcome to Neko Harbour,' he called out. 'Our first landing on the Antarctic mainland.'

Close to our landing point stood a little wooden hut, painted bright red to make it stand out against the natural white, a white so bright it seemed almost *unnatural*. The hut was a refuge erected by the Argentineans in 1949. And what a refuge it must have been to anyone who had run the gauntlet of ice that guarded the Harbour. But now, like the crumbling remains of the station at Whalers' Bay, it was home only to penguins and seals.

The Harbour is named after a Norwegian factory ship which operated there between 1911 and 1924. Looking out into the bay I tried to picture her (tried because I didn't really know what a factory ship looked like) lying there surrounded by the ice, which tolerated her with disinterest as it did now another Norwegian vessel. *Nordnorge* looked suddenly small, disappearing behind one of the aquatic white mountains that patrolled the bay.

Thou rash intruder on our realm below.[xvii]

They stood at the gates of Dis, the threshold to the nether-hell, Dante and his guide. No way to go but onward, for no-one can retreat out of Hell. You can't go back the way you've come. If you do, you may leave Hell, but Hell will not leave you.

And as the demons at the gate appraised them with scorn, 'Thou with us shalt stay,' they say to Virgil.

No.

But did Shackleton, man of words and eloquence and frustrated poet himself, Virgil now to a reluctant Dante, ever think that perhaps he would?

The guide turns to his charge.

'Have no fear, no matter what they do to me. I've been here before.'

Is that why we journey through Hell? So that once we've been there and know the way, we can guide another through?

The paradox of Antarctica began to manifest itself. A place that could be Eden, unsullied, un-fallen, could just as easily be Hell.

Or vice versa.

This terrifying place, with its monstrous inhabitants, was equally the last haven of peace and innocence. But we were banished from Eden.

This is the ice's world, and we really have no business being here.

Back at sea, the image of *Nordnorge* surrounded by the ice continued to haunt me, Nootaikok and his entourage bearing down on her, 'sprits fallen from heaven.'[xviii] According to Milton's theology, the pagan gods were angels who rebelled with Satan. But this is a continent untouched by the Fall. Here, the ice is not evil, cannot be evil. It is merely the proud and indifferent lord of its domain. We are the 'rash intruders' and any wrath it may unleash on us is the result of our own interference. As with all colonising powers, it is when it leaves its own established territory that it commits its atrocities. Although of course it can be equally brutal to those who fail to show proper respect within its borders. And as *Nordnorge* eased her way amongst it en route to that afternoon's landing site I had plenty of time to contemplate.

The ice wooed like Richard of Gloucester, coming to Lady Anne despite having killed those she loved so dearly.

'He is in heaven, where thou shalt never come,' she said of the king Gloucester had so despatched.

'Then let him thank me that holp to send him thither...'

My Beatrice, like Bice di Folco Portinari, preserved forever, at least in memory, in blown youth. In destroying her had the ice given her immortality? Would she otherwise have ended her days in peaceful obscurity at the breakers' yard remembered only as 'the second Olympic-class liner'?

'...for he was fitter for that place than here.'

'And thou unfit for any place but hell.'

Dante's frozen Lake Cocytus at the very centre.

And I would hear it name no other place.

It was an afternoon of brilliant blues and whites. I have always found light to be a truly fascinating phenomenon, ever since I was a child. Neither a wave nor a particle, but both, a dualism that declares itself impossible even as it cannot be denied. The two fundamental building materials of creation, matter and energy, co-existing in that most basic and universal element of existence.

Let there be light.

After all, it was the first created thing.

White light, the light assaulting us now from the ice in the water and the snow on the mountains is the most fascinating, the most impossible, of all. 'White' we consider to be colourless, yet white light separated into its spectrum through a prism contains every colour there is.

Every colour that exists can be found inside the colourless.

Everything in nothing.

We may look at the splendour of the rainbow but we don't believe in colour from the colourless until we have gathered together our science and our logic and our prisms and pulled light apart in a laboratory. Only then do we believe in nature, when we can reproduce it. But now the paradox – the more one knows about light the harder it is to believe in it, it is impossible to deny its existence.

And when those particle-waves of energy that were torn asunder rejoin their diversity comes together in the unity of White Light – purity.

And Antarctica radiates purity to such an extent that we must protect our eyes from it.

This type of light is the holy grail of photography.

This was the reason I had spent a day's wages on that small circular piece of dark glass. Because this light is like something of the Otherworld, of Avalon. It cannot be captured in this form. Not truly.

Light refracts and reflects, angles of incidence, at which it strikes the surface, refraction and reflection at which it leaves, either bending or bouncing back. When light itself can bend, can there be anything that is indisputably constant? Even surrounded by Nature at its most triumphant, most beautiful, I still think in mathematics, in numbers, in sines and cosines, parabolas, hyperbolas and exponentials. It is the way my brain works. And it is the reason why I see the embodiment of divine beauty in a machine. Nature, just like engineering, is full of numbers and is described perfectly by them.

Da Vinci knew that.

And Dante knew that.

Marvelling in the wonders he beholds after his ascent of Mount Purgatory, he watches the gaze of Beatrice, seeing it as though it were a beam of light, reflecting from the surfaces upon which it alighted, 'as from the first a second beam is wont to issue, and reflected upwards rise'[xix] describing perfectly the reflection of light as it might appear idealised. Dante, who rightly has his place among the greatest of poets, sees the mathematics of divine beauty too. Perhaps there is hope for me yet.

But Dante sees more in the light-beam gaze of Beatrice. He goes on to compare the beam of light to 'a pilgrim bent on his return.'[xx] The itinerant has reached the object of his wanderings and however strong the desire to roam, he yearns for home. Or finds that he has been repelled by that which he has sought, just as the light bounces off the reflective surface. But it is possible for both reflection and refraction to occur on contact with certain surfaces. Water, for example. The pilgrim must return, but a part of him remains. Or her.

The Christian faith native to Scotland and Ireland places great value on pilgrimage, on journeying. The idea is simple: the place where one is born is not one's true home. One's true home is what these Celtic Christians called 'the place of one's resurrection,' the place where one encounters the risen Christ and becomes as spiritually complete as is possible while still the soul is still clothed in flesh and blood. Where the Roman church would expect pilgrimages to the shrines of saints and martyrs the Celtic church would encourage its disciples to undertake their *peregrinatio*, a pilgrimage of destination unknown at the outset that would lead them to that place, a place they called 'the place of their resurrection' – their true home.

Dante in Paradise, which was, according to medieval theologian-geographers located on top of a mountain in the southern hemisphere, right about where Antarctica is, 'stared wide-eyed on the sun's face,'[xxi] by following the gaze of his beloved Beatrice. But this pilgrim, this *pellegrin*[8], did not yet rest in the embrace of the embodiment of divine beauty. No supernatural power enabled me to look upon the sun and the blinding purity it awoke here. Only with technology, precision polarising glass covering my eyes, or the lens of my camera, was I permitted a glimpse of what it might look like. But why not? After all, this was Paradise Harbour, named so by the Antarctic pioneers who first landed there.

Today beneath a sun unimpeded by the haze of pollutants tainting more northern skies 'paradise' was a fitting name. But during the southern winter when the sea itself froze and the pack advanced and occupied the entire coast it would be quite a different story.

Paradiso e Inferno.

Heaven and Hell.

I am not the first to see Antarctica at the centre of the Inferno. Apsley Cherry-Gerrard, in *The Worst Journey in the World*, expressed his belief that Dante was right to place ice below fire in his circles of Hell.

And that is true of a fallen world. No paradise on Earth can endure, and that is largely due to the humans who attempt to inhabit it.

Trouble, as ever, in Paradise.

Snakes in the playground.

The demons that creep into tainted paradise. Or that have always been there.

---

[8] In the passage alluded to here, Beatrice's gaze is likened to a *pellegrin* is translated usually as 'pilgrim' but in Sayers translation it is translated as 'peregrine' (falcon). For all Sayers' being my preferred translation, in this instance I prefer 'pilgrim' to 'peregrine' but that is perhaps because it better suits my purpose.

Maybe, rather than being untouched by the Fall, it is the Fall which has made Antarctica what it is, utterly hostile to human life. We have been expelled from Eden and so cannot exist there without conflict, without fighting Nature.

But if this is Eden, what of the demons, the bergs? If this is unsullied creation, are they not a part of the praise that is offered up to God by virtue of its mere existence, as the Psalmist proclaims:

"Let heaven and earth praise Him, the seas and all that move in them."[xxii]

Hail, snow an' ice that praise the Lord: I've met them at their work,
An' wished we had anither route or they anither kirk.[xxiii]

...when suddenly they all ran jostling in again, headlong
Leaving him outside.[xxiv]
As Shackleton parleyed at the gates of a frozen Dis, the demons, the ice, realising perhaps, that it could not hold him, slammed its jaws around his little ship.
No further.
But Dante still had a long way to go.

Paradise Harbour boasted a stone jetty, making landing very civilised when compared to the hang-on-to-Tomas-and-splosh-into-the-water approach we had had so far, and a red hut at the end of it at the base of a hill rising steeply behind it. Like Neko, the base had been constructed by the Argentineans. There is an urban legend (if a continent with no towns can have urban legends) that holds that one base commander at Paradise Harbour set the building on fire after being informed that his tour of duty was to be extended by a year, preferring to commit arson and face the consequences rather than spend another winter in 'Paradise.' And that is true of a fallen world. No 'paradise' on Earth can endure, for us at least. For the natives of Antarctica, harsh though the winters are, no doubt this sheltered bay is still a little knot of paradise.

It was to be about an hour after the landings started before we were to be called, so I settled into my favourite spot beneath the lifeboat, seeking shade so I could take my sunglasses off – I'd noticed at lunchtime that I was getting panda eyes – to watch the Polar Cirkle boats whizzing back and forth, far happier than they had been that morning; discharging their passengers at a jetty appealed to their dignity more than having their noses held against a beach.

After a while I noticed something small and dark appearing on the hill behind the hut, climbing steadily up it. Then another one appeared, and another. I took out the video camera to use it as a telescope. The tiny creatures advancing up the hill were human beings, all in identical red parkas, trudging through the snow up to the summit of the hill. A few of the more daring among them were climbing up a bare outcrop of rock at the very top and waving to the ship before beginning their decent.

By now I wasn't the only observer.

'Are they on their butts?' an American voice next to me asked, whether rhetorically or not I don't know.

I took my face out of the video camera to survey the scene from a wider angle. There were a couple of black dots descending the hill on a far steeper trajectory than those on the way up. I pointed my improvised telescope at them. Yes, there were the people who had just waved to us, sliding down the hill on their backsides.

'Good grief, they are,' I laughed, and passed the camera to the woman next to me so that she could have a look.

The peaceful little harbour with its glorious snowy hills had just been turned into a makeshift adventure playground, swarming with silly tourists.

Paradise lost.

And I was about to join them.

Trudging upwards through the snow, sinking knee-deep with every step, I turned to remark to Dad that my admiration for polar explorers had just crept up a notch and found he wasn't there. He had elected not to join me in my assault on the hill. This was the first time on shore that we hadn't been together. I had never imagined my dad growing old. He wasn't, but finding myself alone in one of these crazy places we both loved awoke in me the realization that one day he would be. I marched on alone. There were others in front of and behind me on the path being worn in the snow, but it seemed as though they weren't really there.

I reached the top of the snow-covered shoulder of the hill and looked around me, down into the harbour below. I could see the little buildings around the jetty and on the tiny headland, but not the ship in the bay. To see the ship I would have to scramble to the top of the outcrop of rock peeping out of the snow from which the first climbers had waved to us. My attempts to climb it met with dismal failure. Wellington boots were not going to get any sort of purchase on the slippery rock and my legs were just too short to reach the ledge that had obviously served as a foothold for those who had already achieved the summit.

I gripped the top of the rock which was about level with my nose and tried for the umpteenth time to step onto the rock face and for the umpteenth time my foot slid right back down as soon as I put my weight on it. I felt the hollowness of something in which I had taken a great deal of pride. I may have been an urban animal for many years, but I could climb. I could stand on the side of a wall, ascend and descend at will, traverse scores of metres without my feet touching the floor. But it was a form of climbing that belonged to the artificial world in which I lived.

I was debating whether or not to take my boots off and try climbing in my socks when I heard a brontine rumble, faint, far away, somewhere in the great white yonder, a rumble that I somehow knew wasn't thunder and was to some inner sense familiar.

Suddenly, I wanted to get down from that lonely height.

Suddenly, I wanted my dad.

90 years in the past and across more than 700 miles of open sea three men trudged across the uncharted interior of South Georgia, depicted in Channel 4's deservedly award-winning masterpiece.

'Perhaps we would get further on our arses!'

Despite the film's impressive authenticity, there is, unfortunately, no evidence in either Frank Worsely's or Shackelton's own published accounts of the crossing of South Georgia that he ever actually said it. Indeed, very little is said in either account about The Slide. But, apparently deeming that a particularly precipitous slope was too steep to descend on foot even by cutting steps in the snow, they made the mutual decision to sit down one behind the other, hold on tight and... go!

Well, if it was good enough for Shackleton, it was good enough for me. And all I had to worry about was crashing into one of the buildings that nestled at the foot of the hill; I wasn't about to go careering off any unknown precipice.

By now so many people had slid down the hill that a half-tunnel, like a toboggan run, had been pressed into the snow. The troubled melancholy that had settled on me evaporated as I sat down and kicked off, tearing down the hillside at a considerably greater speed than that with which I had ascended. I bumped along, the world around me a rushing whiteness until I shot between two exposed faces of rock and hurtled towards the cluster of little red buildings. But my momentum slowed, and I didn't crash. It was almost disappointing.

Dad was waiting for me at the bottom. He hauled me to my feet, both of us laughing. I was a kid in the play-park again with my dad, who would always catch me at the end of the chute and never let me fall (This was in the days before Health and Safety – the chute, roundabout and swings were surrounded by concrete when I was a child). Dad would never grow old.

'Did you hear the glacier calve?' Dad asked when we had composed ourselves.

So that's what it was.

I *had* heard it before, in the high Arctic. We had been 'lucky' enough to witness the event, and certainly lucky that it had only been a small one, although it had rocked our sturdy little icebreaker like a cork in a bathtub.

Somewhere beyond the horizon a monster had been born.

It was open seating for dinner, and a *kalt bord* buffet. I was sporting the bright red of my Stornoway Running Club sweater, which had the club's name printed on a yellow strip across the chest. I wasn't really paying any mind to what I was wearing, until an Irish voice caught my attention.

'Stornoway? You wouldn't happen to know Roddy Cunningham, would you?'

I often get the 'Oh, Stornoway, I've a second cousin twice removed who lives there. Do you know him? His name's Calum' thing. And it's annoying. Stornoway is small, but not that small. However in this case...

'Er, yes, I do. And that's his business partner,' I gestured across the table towards Dad. 'My dad.'

'Jack Kernahan?' the Irishman said.

Dad, bemused shook the offered hand.

'Terry Nolan. I once bought some cages for a fish farm from Roddy.'

Good grief. First Karen-the-Courier and now a random Irishman who'd done business with my dad's current business partner in his previous life (Dad and Roddy are accountants, not suppliers of fish farming equipment. I think it's having such an infamously boring job – thanks be to Monty Python – that makes Dad take such bizarre holidays). Just when you're seeing how vast the globe is you're reminded that it's a small world after all.

It was only by her movement that I spotted her. The daylight was almost gone, and the world outside the window by which I was sitting reading Shackleton's *The Heart of the Antarctic* was turning grey, the falling night gradually mixing daubs of black into the great whiteness that dominated Nature's canvas. She was grey herself, and was it not for her running lights I would have put her down as a trick on the fading light.

'Is that a ship out there?'

Dad peered over the top of *The Forsyte Saga* as I leaned forward, cupping my hands to the glass around my eyes to shut out reflections.

'It is!'

I left the warmth of the lounge and made my way outside, still in my shirtsleeves. Dad put his book down and followed. Out to starboard, sailing purposefully northwards was a ship wearing the gunmetal grey that is the uniform of military vessels the world over. She was just... there, utterly *wrong* among the blankness of the snow-covered hills and headlands yet at the same time making no obvious incursion, at once completely natural and totally alien. I wondered what we looked like to her. *Nordnorge* wore the bold red band around her upper hull that was the distinctive badge of the Hurtigruter and her illuminated funnel was yellow, pale but still no doubt striking against the monochrome backdrop.

Who was she? Possible names swam through mind with a touch of the macabre. *Sheffield. Coventry. Fearless.*

Sir Galahad perhaps? Mortally wounded, she was sent to the bottom not by enemy fire, but by HMS *Onyx*, to serve as war grave. In Arthurian legend her namesake, the noblest and most revered of the knights of the once and future king, was deemed worthy to be taken into Heaven and stand in the presence of Jesus; and her final act was to enter eternity guarding the bones of those who now rested there.

And then the other vessel was gone, melting away into the deepening twilight astern. We had passed starboard to starboard, in itself unconventional, neither ship acknowledging the other's presence. We never found out who she was.

CHAPTER 6
You Shall Not Pass

I was on deck just after seven o'clock. *Nordnorge* had woken me again, not by her movement but by her stillness. The ice was still all around us, but this morning it was wrapped in a thick mist, through which it loomed with menace which that mist barely concealed.

Just give us an excuse…

The bergs like kelpies overside that girn an' turn an' shift
Whaur, grindin' like the Mills o' God, goes by the big South drift.[xxv]

Kelpies. Waterhorses. Sprites of Scottish and Irish mythology that enticed weary travellers to ride on their backs and then galloped off into the loch and drowned them. Oh so many of the faeries of water and sea appear benign. Selkies, Ondines… Sirens, creatures of female form that lured sailors to their deaths with their beauty. And such a thing is the ice. Beautiful but deadly.

Nordnorge lay motionless amongst it – blind monsters that could not sense her presence as long as she remained perfectly still. Like during Dante's descent into the depths of the earth on his journey through Hell, as we travelled further down the globe the Circles grew darker. The mist smudged the harsh outlines of the cliffs and mountains rising on either side of the channel in which we were now stopped, the Neumayer Channel, not dissimilar geologically from the fjords that were the ship's home, where she nimbly negotiated the complex network of shallows and narrows and submerged rocks that form the coast of North Norway, the region whose name she bears. But despite spending more than half her working life above the Arctic Circle, here was an element which she rarely encountered in such strength. Yesterday, perhaps in naïveté, she had parleyed with it. Not today. Today I could have sworn that *Nordnorge* was frightened.

I made my way to the bow. It had snowed overnight and someone had built a tiny snowman on the rail. All was grey, cold and motionless, just me, the ship and the ice, closely packed brash and growlers, the vanguard of the true pack.

We had reach latitude 65 degrees south. We had not even crossed the Antarctic Circle and the ice was turning us back. Here was the frozen lake Cocytus, the very centre of Dante's Hell.

The abyss created when Lucifer fell, the very core of the earth fleeing in terror before him when 'from High Heaven he fell,'[xxvi] excavating his eventual eternal prison as it did so, and erupting into 'that peak of earth'[xxvii] to be ascended by Dante and his guide.

'And so this void was made.'[xxviii]

The Hell that litters the water gives way to the landmass rising exactly where the medieval theologians believed it would.

Theology's Mount Purgatory is geography's Antarctica.

I was quite intrigued by the concept of the 'pre-history of Antarctica.' The commonly understood definition of 'pre-history' is 'that which occurred before there were written records.' So when does history begin on a continent which has no inhabitants to make written records? With its 'discovery' I suppose, but the lecture I had recently attended, entitled 'The Pre-History of Antarctica' had made me wonder what 'discovery' really meant.

One of the ever increasing number of odd things I was learning about Antarctica is that we seem to have always known it to be there. It appears on maps dating back centuries before its discovery as a great landmass, *Terra Australis Incognita*, sometimes spreading out from the tip of South Africa or South America. So certain were 'we' of its existence that George III sent Captain Cook out to look for it, not satisfied that Australia was that great southern landmass. Of course, one could point out that that particular monarch hasn't gone down in history for his sanity, but that doesn't change the fact that Antarctica was there, as yet undiscovered, even if Cook managed to miss it.

(I wish he had found it. My primary school project might have been more interesting if he had.)

But it goes back further. In 500BC, Aristotle proposed that there must be a great landmass in the southern hemisphere to balance that in the north otherwise the world would topple over. That may make us in our technologically and scientifically advanced times think, 'Bless his little cotton socks,' but it was still an intuitive reality, that there must be an Antarctica. (And before we allow ourselves to become condescending we must remember that we owe most of our scientific prowess to the Greeks, and much of that to Aristotle.) Maybe the mediaeval theologians had something when they proposed that the Garden of Eden was on top of a mountain on a continent in the southern hemisphere – it would have made sense. We appear to have a 'racial memory' of it and so 'know it to be there.' But we were banished from Eden and so are unable to return there, no matter how hard we try. It must therefore be somewhere so far away and inaccessible, like on an island (albeit a very large island) on the other side of the world, that no-one in the (known) world has ever been there.

I try not to think about the Piri Reis Map.

It makes my head hurt.

Piri Reis was a Turkish admiral who, in 1513, more than two hundred years before the 'discovery' of Antarctica, produced a map which shows the coastline of the Antarctic continent as it would appear free of ice. Piri Reis said of his map that it was drawn from older portolans, books which contain maps and descriptions of coastlines – harbours, river-mouths and coastline features visible from the sea and such like used by the ancients for navigation.

As I trawl the internet, checking my facts on dates et cetera for the Piri Reis Map before I commit myself to writing my skimming gaze catches on a sentence: 'Recent aerial photographs have shown clearly circular structures or pyramidal formations that lie beneath the ice of Antarctica.' And the damage is done. On the Information Superhighway I have crashed and burned. Is this how Eve felt? Is this the Fall, the assimilation of unwanted knowledge that cannot be unlearned? But the page has not reproduced these aerial photographs. So I call up Google, I begin to search... I stop myself deliberately. Yes, this is the Fall, the desire for forbidden knowledge, for foolish knowledge, but the more you know the more you want to learn. I have found no reproductions of aerial photographs of pyramids beneath the ancient ice of Antarctica. I am still free to choose not to believe this nonsense. And we see pyramids everywhere, don't we, even on the surface of Mars. If there can be pyramids on Mars, why not on Antarctica? And if they turn out to be the product of light and shadow, altitude and angle of the camera on Mars, then that's what they are on Antarctica too. Pyramids are an icon of civilisation, and Antarctica, like Mars, is just too big for us to be able to accept that it has never subjugated to 'civilisation.' And so we see pyramids in the wilderness.

But the Piri Reis Map disturbs me. Antarctica free of ice and snow in lost antiquity. I think I want it to be a fake, but I don't see how it can be. It surfaced in 1929, before satellite imagery had made our modern maps with which it has been compared. But the part of my faith that never left Sunday School wants the mediaeval theologians to be right – that the Garden of Eden was a real place, and it was in Antarctica, and that somehow one of the first people sailed around it and mapped it even though he couldn't land because all humanity had been banished from Eden, and that somehow the portolan he wrote was passed down and down and down until it was given to Piri Reis who drew the map...

But I also want there to be Unicorns and Dragons fighting epic battles in the Scottish mountains and Welsh valleys, and there to be Liverbirds gazing out up the Mersey waiting for the safe return from the sea of the menfolk of Liverpool.

At the other end of the world, one of *Nordnorge*'s extended family crosses the

Arctic Circle going north every day, and another going south, a silly but fun ceremony made out of it for the tourists involving one of the crew dressing up as Neptune and pouring ladles-full of iced water down people's necks. Looking out at the chilling vista before us I couldn't imagine anything so frivolous happening here if the ice should permit a visitor to proceed as far as the Antarctic Circle. And this was not our privilege. We were here on its terms and respect was demanded.

Nordnorge didn't seem to like it either. Any icebreaker would almost certainly have advanced, here on the edge of the pack at least the stronger of the two combatants, forcing the ice to yield; but at Ice Class C *Nordnorge*'s weaponry is defensive only. Any attempt at attack would be foolish. Suicidal.

Slowly, she began to rotate about her vertical axis, like a compass needle seeking north. At home in Norway, this manoeuvre is usually executed at the end of a narrow fjord, a slightly cocky demonstration of the marvellous dexterity of these ships, built for the tight confines of the Norwegian coastline. In the Trollfjord it was a party piece; in the Lamaire Channel, it was a means of escape. When she had turned a full 180 degrees, *Nordnorge*'s engines thrummed to life, but cautiously, and she left the ice the undisputed master of all it chooses to hold.

It chose to hold *Endurance*, Sir Ernest Shackleton's ship. In November of 1915, in the Weddell Sea, on the other side of the Peninsula from where *Nordnorge* had humbly turned around, acknowledged the ice as lord, and left it unchallenged, the ice's grip tightened one final time around a presumptuous little vessel that had not shown such respect. *Endurance* had been beset in the ice since January and after months of torture it finally decided to kill its victim. Her groans of agony a warning to her master and crew, Shackleton ordered that the ship be abandoned, landing all they could onto the ice's shifting surface, including three of the ship's small boats. The executioner's grip was tightened by pressures building up hundreds of miles away. It killed slowly. The humans had plenty of time. But the time came at last.

'She's going, boys,' said the Boss.

And the ice closed over her as though she had never been there.

Nordnorge headed north, out of hell, 'for better waters... leaving that ocean of despair.'[xxix] Away from hell, but at the same time away from Paradise.

> *And ice mast-high came floating by*
> *As green as emerald.*

How did Coleridge know? He was writing at the end of the eighteenth century. Antarctica was still hypothetical Cook had after all, as I later learned, managed to sail right around it and miss it) and there hadn't been enough significant

Arctic exploration to allow him to extrapolate from accounts of it. Yet it was as though he had been there. Been *here*.

> *The ice was here, the ice was there*
> *The ice was all around:*
> *It cracked and growled, and roared and howled...*

Ice is noisy. The accounts of Shackleton in the south and Nansen in the north describe the eerie and disturbing audio assaults they endured, particularly at night. Easy to imagine, then, that it is indeed a living thing, the embodiment of some sort of spirit of the air, neither of heaven nor hell. Did such a spirit follow our wake northwards now, from the land of mist and snow, as one had the Ancient Mariner, the spirit that 'loved the bird that loved the man that shot it with his bow'?

Why *did* the Ancient Mariner shoot the albatross?

Many great literary minds have pondered the question in vain, for no explanation is given in the poem. Perhaps that's just it - there was no reason. It was a random act of violence. Set against the poem's undeniable spiritual themes, perhaps it is representative of Sin, which just exists within fallen humankind, and hangs about our neck like... well, the image of the Ancient Mariner and the albatross is so ingrained in our culture that it is instantly recognisable as a depiction of bearing the consequences of some terrible deed.

What of the Ancient Mariner's shipmates, who alternately condemn, condone, then condemn again the 'hellish thing' the Mariner had done? In their superstition, they saw the imprint of their circumstances everywhere. The albatross was a 'bird of good omen' because when it appeared the ice began to part, the winds grew favourable and the ship was able to make her way through - what the Mariner did was wrong. Then the mist and fog that had surrounded them cleared, they concluded that the albatross had indeed *brought* the unfavourable weather, and that what the Ancient Mariner did was right. How true of human inconstancy. Maybe Hamlet, in his feigned madness, was onto something when he said that 'nothing is good nor bad but thinking makes it so.' And sadly also how true of the darker side of human nature, weighted towards selfish self-preservation - when 'the Albatross begins to be avenged' they blame the Ancient Mariner. The need for a scapegoat. It is as old as Sin itself, ever since Adam told the Lord that Eve gave him the fruit.

Human inconstancy. And superstition. Even more than two hundred years after the Rime was composed, whether we like it or not, despite all our professed belief in Science and its rationalisation of and explanations for everything that happens in the cosmos, we are a superstitious species.

When judgement comes, it falls upon the entire crew, guilty by complicity. Surely this must give us pause. That by justifying and then considering the crime or evil actions of another to be the 'right thing to do' we are as guilty of that act as the perpetrator.

The suffering crew change their minds again, and now deem the Mariner wicked, condemning him for his deed. But now it is too late.

Where does that leave us in a day and age where many of the traditional 'vices' are considered to be virtues? Where those who exhibit these new virtues are admired and hailed as gods of the post-modern world? When Greed has become Ambition and has trampled upon Compassion and in so doing is quietly suffocating humanity. When Wrath is permitted to control rather than be controlled, and is called instead Strength. And when Sloth is not only tolerated but rewarded and 'Won't' is redefined as 'Can't.'

But to return to the original question - why did the Ancient Mariner shoot the albatross? According to William Wordsworth, it was because he suggested it.

A bit of an anti-climax, isn't it?

I was dismayed to discover that Coleridge had been addicted to opium. I took a walk once in Highgate that passed by the house where he had lived as a 'patient/lodger' of Dr James Gillman, under a sort of self-imposed house arrest, in the hope that he would be cured.

Of course, there is the sorrow that a man should be so blighted with all the tragedy that ensues, but there is also a tragedy for literature. The nightmare scenes that leap from one horror to another would seem likely to be the product of an over-stimulated imagination, leaving one to wonder - is this genius or a drug-induced frenzy of the mind? If it were not for Coleridge's affliction, would The Rime of the Ancient Mariner have been written? Almost certainly it would, for it grew out of a dream related to Coleridge by a friend which featured a 'skeleton ship.' But all its wondrous strange, macabre and magnificent, awful and awesome imagery - would that have come about? Is it conceivable that this masterpiece, in all its tortured glory, only exists because of a man's suffering?

'...like the poet needs the pain,' sang Jon Bon Jovi.

There are all too many addicts, but there is only one Rime. Maybe the vivid, vicious vistas of the Rime are the opium talking, but opium cannot use words. To turn such an onslaught on the mind's eye into words, words so sublime as those commanded by Coleridge here takes genius. And thus is made triumph out of tragedy. For it is only by the words that we can sojourn with the Ancient Mariner through his world of dreams and visions, sail his ocean, mourn with him the death of the albatross.

Does this perhaps give the Rime a greater dignity?

A sadder and a wiser man he woke the morrow morn.

Dante is not the only one to find Hell in the ice and Purgatory in the southern hemisphere, although the Ancient Mariner's South Pole was an ocean. What else could the Mariner's torments amount to - a murder done, and raging tortures and guilt visited upon him in which he finds himself unable to pray.

> *And a thousand, thousand slimy things*
> *Lived on, and so did I...*
> *...And yet I could not die*

The private hell of the Ancient Mariner rings of John's apocalyptic vision on the Isle of Patmos, when he foresaw a time when under the wrath of the Lamb, men 'shall desire to die, and death shall flee from them.'[xxx]
 And as he sails northwards he find that after blessing God's creatures that he sees all around him he is able to pray again,

> *And from my neck so free*
> *The Albatross fell off and sank*
> *Like lead into the sea*

Surely this is the sin purged?

***

Deception Island, Neko Harbour and Paradise Bay easily left one with the impression that the Antarctic Peninsula has been abandoned by humans, or that they have been expelled from it. But Port Lockroy is still operated by the British Antarctic Survey, a little outpost that looks like the sort of place the Starship *Enterprise* might find and have to break the news to its inhabitants that half a century has passed.
 Sounding more like a village on the west coast of Scotland than a harbour in the Antarctic named after a Frenchman[9], Port Lockroy differed somewhat from our previous landing sites. The ubiquitous red huts do not feature – the buildings are black with a smart red band below the roofs, putting me in mind of the Hurtigrute livery – there is a resident human presence, and tourists are actually helping with the research being conducted there rather than just making a nuisance of themselves. It was also our first landfall, still hundreds miles from the Falklands, on historically contested territory.
 Port Lockroy was used amicably by whalers of sundry nationalities from the first time the surrounding bay was used in around 1904 until the early 1930s, and then seems to have been left alone for over ten years. An Argentinean claim on the harbour and surrounding territory provoked a

---

[9] Eduouard Lockroy was vice-president of the French Chamber of Deputies in 1903 and helped secure funding for the expedition which discovered Port Lockroy.

response of 'No, it's ours!' from the British, who moved in to remove all Argentinean national identifiers and established a meteorological station there, imaginatively named 'Base A.' The fact that it was a French expedition which found the natural harbour in the first place seems to have been conveniently forgotten. But the base is still staffed by the British Antarctic Survey. Not as a weather station, those operations ceased in 1962, but as a museum. However, an experiment is being conducted there, one in which the tourists lend a hand, whether they realise it or not.

The effect of the presence of humans on the local gentoo penguins is under investigation. The little island on which the base is built is divided by a fence and on one side the penguins are isolated from visitors to the base. Those penguins on the other side have the dubious honour of being allowed to interact with the tourists, although 'interacting' in this case appeared to mean standing there looking miserable while people in red anoraks point cameras at them.

All the penguins at Port Lockroy look miserable. Even the one standing by the Union Flag outside the base. He looks as though he's been told to stand there and look patriotic. Is this down to the effect of tourism, that penguins have decided to pander to their visitors by standing dutifully if unenthusiastically beneath the banner of the country that has built a nest on their little island? They'd even brought their weather with them today, dull and damp and generally rotten. This probably wasn't helping the penguins' mood. And I wondered if we smelled as bad to them as they did to us.

The museum resides in the original station hut, Bransfield House, and was restored to its 1960s condition by the UK Antarctic Heritage Trust in 1996. There is even a full-length portrait of Marilyn Monroe on the back of the generator-shed door. I was more interested in the generator itself.

It was wonderful, this snapshot of life during that scientifically pioneering era. It's just sad to think that the only reason it's there is that Britain, like a spoiled child, only decided they wanted the harbour because someone else did.

There was one more task to be undertaken before leaving this tiny speck of civilisation, for civilisation it can reasonably be called – Port Lockroy has a post office, a service championed as the centre of rural life now under threat in so many parts of the UK.

'It serves a community of six people,' says the imaginary minister for saving public money, advocating its closure. 'And even they are not there all the year round.'

'But they can't exactly hop on a bus to the next town,' retorts the equally imaginary lobbyist campaigning to keep it open. 'And as many as three hundred can pass through in a single day.'

Today was one of those days.

The Post Office at Port Lockroy might serve a community considerably smaller than those under threat at home, but it probably has the largest catchment area in the world.

The idea entered my head that maybe Antarctica isn't so different after all.

The presence, however unlikely, of the Post Office made it mandatory that we perform that solemn duty of tourists the world over and send postcards.

I had still been struggling with mine, all purchased in the onboard gift shop, as *Nordnorge* continued to pick her way through Purgatory after breakfast. The gift shop sadly was doing a roaring trade in disposable cameras due to the misplacement of those belonging to the victims of the baggage incident. I'd now decided that never again was I putting my camera in my hold luggage, as not only had it been in danger of being left in London but it had narrowly escaped accidental adoption by a random Argentinean. I was finding that putting any one of my experiences so far into a few sentences stripped it of what made it worth writing home about in the first place. Tourists have not only infiltrated the last uninhabited continent, but they can now belittle it by reducing it to half a six-by-four postcard. Helping with the experiment on the penguins hardly makes up for it.

I settled for raving about the ship, my friends would be expecting that, and promising to regale them with great tales of my adventures upon my return. But on one I wrote simply 'Job 38:29-30.'[10] This was on one of the two pages Shackleton kept from the Bible Queen Alexandra had presented to the Expedition. I knew the recipient would appreciate it.

That Bible was rescued from the ice to which it had been abandoned by a man hailing from the same hard-bitten old lump of rock that I do. Thomas MacLeod, although possibly born in Glasgow, grew up in Stornoway, in a building in Point Street, notable in my day for being a chip shop. When he joined Shackleton's Imperial Trans-Antarctic Expedition in 1914 he was already a veteran of polar exploration. He had journeyed to the southern polar regions before with Captain Scott on his final expedition. Being one of the ship's crew rather than a member of the Expedition proper MacLeod returned with *Terra Nova*, the ship, to New Zealand, leaving Scott and his party to prepare for the race they would lose along with their lives. His experiences after the loss of *Endurance* didn't put him off either. He returned to the Antarctic with Shackleton in 1921 aboard *Quest*, the expedition from which Shackleton himself would not return.

That verse was also marked by a tiny dried flower in the Bible received by Thomas Kernahan when he joined the Navy, just a boy, not yet fifteen. When his son passed it on to his daughter, he said to her,

'It's as if he was speaking to you from beyond the grave.'

---

[10] 'Out of whose womb came the ice? And the hoary frost of heaven, who hath gendered it? The waters are hid as with a stone, and the face of the deep is frozen.'

I never met my grandfather, but so many times my grandmother had said, 'Oh, he would have loved you.

He had marked another page as well, in the hymnary at the back. A hymn by Alfred, Lord Tennyson.

Sunset and evening star
And one clear call for me
And may there be no meaning of the bar
When I put out to sea
But such a tide as moving seems asleep
Too full for sound and foam
When that which drew from out the boundless deep
Turns again home

Twilight and evening bell
And after that the dark
And may there be no sadness of farewell
When I embark
Though from out our bourne of time and place
The flood may bear me far
I hope to see my Pilot face to face
When I have crossed the bar.

As do I.

And manyothers besides. Among them Telegraphist Haig Kernahan.

We slid through the water in a near-whiteout, the snow and ice on the land becoming one with the heavy white sky. Ice blink, perhaps, the glare on the underside of clouds that betrayed the ice's presence even when it was beyond the range of human sight. Changes in the colour of the sky had been one of the most basic, and heavily relied upon, means of navigation used by early explorers venturing into the polar regions, the dark underside of the clouds of the sky over water showing them where it was ice-free. Or at least, where it was not dominant.

Everything around us seemed to absorb sound, the water, the land, that searing sky, everything, like the anechoic chambers I sometimes use at work to test satellites' electromagnetic properties. Again, as with the 'wind tunnel' in Neptune's Bellows, Nature was presenting us with her version of what we take such pride in having achieved by our technology.

The object of our little cruise in the Polar Cirkle boats appeared suddenly, dark against the prevalent white. I had never seen a wreck before except in photographs or on film. Abandoned vessels that had fallen into such a state of decay that they were unsalvageable, yes, but never a wreck, a ship whose life

71

had been cut short either by accident or design. She was a Norwegian factory ship, Tomas had told us. Her name was *Governen*. She had caught fire, almost paradoxically one of the worst things that can happen at sea, surrounded by water; that water will sooner kill you than put the fire out.

She was not sunk completely. Her bow was exposed, as though she was trying to haul herself up from the bottom, like some undead thing fighting its way out of the tomb. I gazed with a fascination I found disturbing even as I scrutinised the tragic scene, a combination of horror, revulsion and heartbreak, with just a little forensic curiosity as an engineer, distressed by what I saw, yet feeling as though to look away would dishonour her somehow. I don't know if any human life was lost aboard her. I didn't think to ask.

Through my sorrow, my thoughts, inevitably, were drawn to a shattered hull lying two and a half miles below the surface of the North Atlantic, noble and upright on the edge of eternity. Torn in two, her stern imploded, slowly consumed by the ocean…but it's better than this.

They always right themselves at a certain depth. It's a quirk of hydrodynamics, reduced by our science to numbers and equations. I prefer to think of it as God allowing them some final dignity.

Returning to the ship, *Nordnorge* had never seemed so alive. Her lights burned brightly, calling her little boats home, and her yellow, flood-lit funnel stood out as a beacon of warmth and colour in the cold white. After my second hot shower of the day – good grief, what would Shackleton and co have had to say about that? – and settled in the café with a mug of steaming, milky tea to accelerate the thawing process, I still felt a pall hanging over us. The melancholy that had settled on the ship after her encounter with the ice this morning had been lifted during our visit to Port Lockroy, if for no reason other than to laugh at the miserable penguins, but the afternoon's morbid expedition had allowed it to return, despite the ship's cheerful warmth, abundant hot water and tea and coffee free and on tap. These waters were not safe.

***

Cardiff Bay.

 All endings have a beginning.

 Approaching Roald Dahl Plass I pass a stylised effigy gazing out to the waters which he crossed as he began that final journey. It took a moment to register, but it's now obvious who the 'Scott' of 'Scott Harbour' is. The road sign fills my vision as I run towards it, leaving briefly behind the immense water tower, cascading perpetually between heaven and earth. And below…

 Thou rash intruder…

 From these stones horizons sing, and now I know what that means.

 It is the Cardiff Half Marathon. Edinburgh, the marathon for which I had been training while I was in the Antarctic, is now a memory. I have never run so fast in my life. And in seven miles I will smash my previous personal best time by nine and a half minutes. I've never felt so alive.

The beating of my heart, fast but steady, pumping the blood to my legs, to my hamstrings, calves, quadriceps. It makes its journey through veins and arteries. There is no fatigue. Each beat of my heart is in perfect time with each breath that I take, filling every sac in my lungs, injecting oxygen into the blood pumped to my legs, to my hamstrings...

The life is in the blood.

But what resides in the heart and mind and soul of one for whom there will be no tomorrow?

If it be now, 'tis not to come.
If it be not to come it will be now.
If it be not now yet it will come.
The readiness is all.[xxxi]

A figure marches towards infinity, noble, tragic. Hamlet in a snowstorm. Captain Oates, his course set for the undiscovered country on an undiscovered continent. Special providence in the fall of a sparrow, alone, on the frozen waste as the end of the world.

The end began here, just as surely as the end which came to the others in the tent. When death is inevitable, does it make any difference whether one simply waits for it or walks out into the storm to meet it head on?

I think perhaps it does.

'I am just going outside and I may be some time. [xxxii]

The cycle continues through my circulatory system, heart and lungs working to go on delivering oxygen, vital for human life, to limbs that should be exhausted but instead are flying.

The oxygen is vital, but it is the blood that carries it.

The life is in the blood.

'The heart will cease to beat
For all things must die. [xxxiii]

The water tower approaches again to my left as the route swings round the back of the Millennium Centre.

The fall of a sparrow.

God is gracious.

'When your back's against the wall and no hope is left, get down on your knees and pray for Shackleton.' But sometimes there comes a point when all you can do is walk out into the blizzard.

It is easier to face the unfaceable when one has chosen to do so.

73

'What do you want to go to Antarctica for?' a colleague of mine had asked. 'It's all white.'

Admiralty Bay on King George Island proved just how wrong that notion was. Just as the evening sun had released such glorious colour on Deception Island, the sun still climbing over Arctowski Station called forth their equally splendid morning counterparts.

Dante, in the Garden of Eden atop Mount Purgatory, looked into the sun for 'There much is granted which is here denied.' And indeed it is denied. Even here, in this paragon of Eden. For we must be protected from the purity of Nature here, light of heaven unsullied by contamination of earth. We can only look upon this light, the epitome of unspoilt Nature by shielding eyes with our technology, our polarising lenses and filters. Light that we, as human beings are forbidden to look upon.

In order to look upon the brilliance of Heaven, Dante, in the care of his beloved Beatrice at last, follows her gaze as she faces the sun.

Mine does not.

Face the sun, that is.

Her bow points due North. But towards no sun, as did the bow of gallant *Nordnorge* in that antipodean ocean, only towards the frozen womb that gave birth to her killer.

I am standing on the starboard promenade deck. Mary steams westwards. She knows. I know she knows, the burden of love this tiny human creature bears as she carries her on her pilgrimage. A chart of the North Atlantic Ocean is spread out on the cabin floor several decks below, the course from Southampton plotted and scrutinized carefully every few hours, after the 'kid with the GPS' has taken a new reading. It's early morning, just after six, a mist suspended in the air; the North Atlantic is wearing its true colours, a blue-grey as deep as the ocean itself that smudges into the lighter sky on the southern horizon. The sky wraps itself in clouds as though to protect its modesty, hiding the sunrise that lies behind us. Twenty years ago, to this very day, a six-year-old girl was allowed to stay up until ten o'clock to watch a programme about a ship that sank a long time ago. And learning that the QM2 was making this Westbound Transatlantic... I did the calculations. That she would bring me to this spot on this day... was it all arranged especially for me by the One who controls the oceans and the tides? A lot of dead-reckoning has been employed, but Mary is so steady in her course that I know exactly where we are. I watch the GPS. It approaches. I check my compass and set my gaze south. I cross Longitude 49° 56'W[11]. For that tiny moment, we face each other.

---

[11] The commonly quoted final resting place of Titanic is 41° 46'N, 50° 14'W. This however is her final reported position on the surface. The co-ordinates of the wreck site are 41° 44'N, 49° 56'W

The Stygian gloom of the fringes of the ice's realm behind us and yesterday's visit to that terrible open grave seemingly forgotten, the Polar Cirkle boats gambolled in the bright light, the calm, ice-free waters of the bay permitting them the freedom they so enjoyed. Even with no passengers they continued to circle *Nordnorge* and each other, their lone pilots standing in the stern, from which their little Norwegian flags fluttered proudly, accompanied on one by a strangulated soft-toy penguin that served as a mascot.

Arctowski is a Polish research station established in 1977. A Norwegian flag, considerably larger than those displayed by the Polar Cirkle boats, had been raised perhaps in honour of today's visitors, or maybe for some other reason entirely. Not that I could think what that could possibly be. It would be an astonishing coincidence.

The main field of study here is ecology, essentially life in its environment. And here, for all this environment's reputation for hostility to it, *is* life.

Spread out in front of the station, like the manicured lawn of a stately home, a carpet of moss enjoys the sun, where 'Keep off the grass' strictly applies. Surrounded by glaciers, those great sterilisers of continents, is a little pocket of vitality, plant life of living jade and emerald with animals sustained by the freezing sea and a little community of eleven human beings. Antarctica never ceases to surprise.

If one such surprise had been the Post Office at Port Lockroy, then Antarctica had another up her metaphorical sleeve at Arctowski. It was here that we found the Tourist Information Centre. A wooden sign with the designation carved onto it pointed to a little round building, also of wood, with a conical roof, the sort that one would expect to see wisps of smoke drifting out of the apex. It looked very new. I peered in at the window, but it appeared to be closed. I wondered if it was some sort of a joke.

Interlude

Now novelty and frivolity lie behind. For most, we are leaving the object of this voyage, the Southern Continent; but for us, for me, and you who travel with me, the journey has just begun. All your raconteuse has shown you, is only the beginning. All these things that we have seen are heavy with the weight of the past, but what is past is prologue and now we sail boldly into history, my ship 'carving her course and singing as she sails.'[xxxiv] But does she sing with joy or does she sing a dirge? Or a shanty, a song of the sea that mourns a life left behind on land even though the singer would never leave the sea. 'Landfalls and departures, leaving home, coming home, beginnings and endings...'[12] So,

---

[12] The Onedin Line, 'Stand By To Come About.' James. He blew up a sheet of pack ice ('Ice

dear Reader, I ask, do you follow in my wake for the sake of the story, for I have been assured that I *can* tell a story, 'follow in light cockle-shells,'[xxxv] vessels unsuited for the wilds of this ocean of triumphant tragedy and its islands of tragic triumph. If so 'tempt not the deep'[xxxvi] for thus far I hope my tale has done justice to its pitiless ferocity, 'turn back and seek the safety of the shore'[xxxvii] for now we are 'pointed to the Bears'[xxxviii] and 'oceans as yet undared my vessel dares.'[xxxix]

No? I thought not. Your ship is seaworthy, ocean-worthy, storm-worthy. I know you would not have set out as my companion on this voyage if it were not.

And remember, the ocean is worth the storm.

CHAPTER 7
Elephant Island

Calculations and clock watching began after returning to the ship. Next on the itinerary was Elephant Island, nothing to do with the large grey animals to be found in Africa or India, but rather it takes its name from sea elephants, which were abundant there at the turn of the twentieth century, when names were being handed out in the south Polar Regions. Before Shackleton and his crew arrived in April 1916 no one had ever set foot on it, with the stow-away Blackborrow being the first to sit down on it, even if he were not the first to stand on it[13]. And we weren't going to get there before dark.

Standing looking out over *Nordnorge's* forecastle willing her onwards I found myself wondering as I often have done before and since what went through Shackleton's mind after *Endurance* foundered. They were at sea without a ship.

After the loss of *Endurance*, Shackleton was left with the gargantuan task of getting twenty-seven men, plus himself, home. Over the course of five months they drifted 600 miles with the ice, allowing it to carry them and their camp, which they named 'Patience', north. At last the ice reached it natural boundary. Outwith these limits it was weaker but no less dangerous. Unable to support the rag-tag band of human parasites that had attached themselves to its surface it was now in a position to throw them off and send them sprawling into the sea. So they took to the boats, boats that they had salvaged from *Endurance* and dragged some way across the surface of the ice itself, each named after a

---

and Fire'). If he was real, he'd be my hero too.

[13] Of course, this may be artistic licence, but as always the quality of Channel 4's script makes it highly probable that this is true.

(1)*Nordnorge* (right) in Stornoway Harbour, as the island ferry, *Isle of Lewis*, approaches the adjacent berth.

(2) Left: HSBC, 'the world's local bank' (just don't try to change sterling to pesos), behind the monument to the May Revolution of 1810, Buenos Aires

PLATE 1

(3) Top: What more is there to say?
Above: ((4) Right) The Prison Train at Museo Maritimo y ex Presidio de Ushuaia and ((5) left) the author on board.
(6) Left: Ah, on the shores of the Drake Passage…   **PLATE 2**

(7) Above: The cruise ship responsible for chartering the End of the World Train ((8) below, although Not in Service), watched over by two Argentinean naval vessels.

PLATE 3

(9) Above: Rounding the Horn (and trying to stay on my feet!)

Above: Going ashore: Dad dons his gear in the car deck ((10) left), and ((11) right) a Polar Cirkle boat discharges its occupants ashore.

PLATE 4

(12) Above: *Thou rash intruder on our realm below…*
Nordnorge at Niko Harbour

(13) Above: Tabular iceberg near Paradise Harbour

PLATE 5

(14) Above: Intrepid explorers climb the hill behind Paradise Harbour
and ((15) below) the prize, the view from the top.

PLATE 6

(16) Above: *Nordnorge* approaches the edge of the pack ice, latitude 65° south.

PLATE 7

(17) Left: at Arctowski Base a signpost lists the distances to destinations such as Krakow, Warsaw and Moscow. London, New York and Paris do not feature!

(18) Above:Elephant Island takes form from out of the haze that merges sea with sky on the horizon.

PLATE 8

(19) Above: Small iceberg in a field of brash ice and growlers.

(20) Above: approaching Grytviken
(21) Below: two Polar Circkle boat make for the shore next to abandoned whalers *Petrel* and *Albatross*.

PLATE 9

(22) Left: From a respectful distance: Shackleton's final resting place, framed in the foreground by the cross marking a whaler's grave.

(23) Above: Shackleton's Highway: the route followed by Shackleton, Creane and Worsley as they approached Stromness whaling station after their crossing of South Georgia.

PLATE 10

(24) Above: a tinge of irony. Such effort is made to preserve the 'pristine' Antarctic environment, yet the sub-Antarctic islands are so filth-ridden, despite the statement made on the oil storage unit ((25) below), that approach to structures is forbidden.

PLATE 11

(26) Above: Polar Cirkle boats head back to Nordnorge, as yet unknown to be 'slightly captive' in Stromness Harbour!

(27) Left: Polar Cirkle boats return their charges to the mother ship.

PLATE 12

(28) Right: brute force is used to try to free the seized anchor chain-stop.

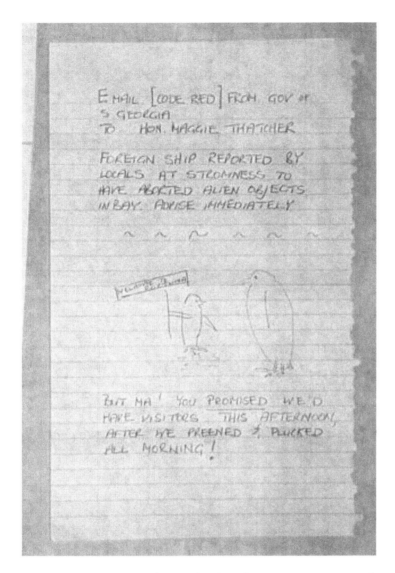

(29) Above: Posted on the ship's notice-board. One passenger sees the funny side of the 'anchor incident' and resulting cancellation of the Fortuna Bay landing.

PLATE 13

(30) Above: Fitting the spare anchor, Port Stanley

(31) Left: The Liberation Monument, Stanley.

(32) Below: Not something one is likely to find in the 'mother country.'

PLATE 14

(33) Above: The Union Flag flies defiantly on the shores of the 'Islas Malvinas'

(34) Above: a young albatross stretches his wings, now losing their down as he approaches adulthood.

PLATE 15

(38) Above: God's providence is our inheritance.

(35) Above: Tomas returns to the ship after clearing customs in Buenos Aires.

PLATE 16

(37) Below: Stornoway Harbour iced over, December 2010

benefactor of the expedition: *Dudley Docker*, *Stancomb-Wills* and *James Caird*. *Endurance* was no more, unable to protect her fragile, perishable cargo of humanity any longer, and now it fell to her three tiny daughters to deliver them to safety.

They set sail for Elephant Island.

It makes it sound so easy.

King George Island is the northern-most of the South Shetland Islands, a little further from the Peninsula than most of the islands in the archipelago and Elephant Island is further out still. We were in comparable starting positions, *Nordnorge* the same distance southwest of Elephant Island as Shackleton had been southeast, three points of an equilateral triangle with the island at its apex. Soon after leaving Arctowski the horizon was empty, and remained so as the daylight faded. We sailed for about six hours before we reached it. Shackleton's little fleet sailed for six days. It is only when you're out here that you get a true sense of just how vast this continent and its surrounding ocean actually are. It was entirely possible that they would sail between Elephant Island and 'neighbouring' Clarence Island and not see either of them.

There was still just enough daylight to see Elephant Island when it appeared on the horizon at about 8pm.

Dad had been outside somewhere. I was with Shackleton in *The Heart of the Antarctic* again, but again only from the comfort of the lounge that ran along the corridor of Deck 4. Dad came in, leaned over my shoulder, the cold still radiating from his jacket, and said quietly, 'It's there.'

I followed him out, nipping into my cabin on the way for my jacket and, more out of habit than anything else, my camera bag. The decks were almost deserted. Half the passengers were having dinner and most of the others were tucked away in the observation lounge, which, when darkness descends, isn't the best place for observing.

'Over there.'

He pointed to a strip of horizon off the port bow. The shape crouching there wasn't really any darker than the surrounding grey sky, just more... three-dimensional.

I used the video camera as a telescope again. The auto-focus protested, the distance and the predominant grey stretching it to the limits of its capabilities. Yes, the something was definitely an island. I passed it to Dad. He squinted through it for a moment, picking out as I had the slightly darker faces of cliffs and shadows of glaciers. Even at this distance it looked utterly forbidding. Yet this was salvation to Shackleton and his men. Once again, the fusion of heaven and hell in the wildest place on earth.

Cruise operators in the Antarctic do not advertise landings at Elephant Island. Some of them say they'll try, but even in the twenty-first century, with a sturdy mother ship standing by and outboard motors on the landing craft a landing can rarely be achieved such are the currents, cliffs, submerged rocks and sheer force of the surrounding ocean. And Shackleton and his men did it in three rowing boats.

We grinned at each other. Elephant Island. And my Dad saw it first!

A couple of other passengers walked by, looking at me like I was mad, filming an apparently empty horizon. It was frustrating – as we drew closer the light got worse. But before it departed we were able to see the island as it is, heavily glaciated with the pointy mountains that give its alter ego in the north, Spitzbergen, its name. We decided to go indoors and check the GPS co-ordinates displayed for the benefit of passengers on a screen next to the courier's desk on Deck 4. The latitude and longitude were kosher, but the little graphic of the ship seemed to sail over land when amongst a dense gathering of islands. Which there certainly wasn't out here, so at the moment it was all right. Loud Englishman, who had loudly told his neighbour on the plane to Madrid that *Nordnorge* was an icebreaker, was now loudly telling someone that we were nowhere near Elephant Island. He saw us gazing out the window; once you knew it was there it demanded that you keep looking at it.

'What have you seen?' Loud Englishman asked loudly. 'A whale?'

Dad turned his head and replied over his shoulder, 'No. Elephant Island.'

We both stood away from the window to allow him to see. He moved forward and peered out, as though he expected to be able to tell us not to be silly.

If this had been a movie you'd have said, 'Yeah, right, like that's going to happen.'

The intercom chimed.

'Ladies and gentlemen, now visible on the port side is Elephant Island...'

It was completely dark by the time we had rounded Cape Valentine, the north-east extremity of the island where Shackleton and his men first landed, and sailed on to Cape Wild, named for Shackleton's second-in-command, where twenty-two of the twenty-eight men would await rescue for four months. After an announcement made over the tannoy we all piled out on deck as the ship's searchlight sought out the little beach. This was beyond the camera's capabilities. Whether he ever actually said it or not, but attributed to him in Channel 4's *Shackleton*, I have to agree with Frank Hurley, a prince among men and a warrior with the camera, 'Sometimes the eye is good enough.'

And what a sight it was – the pitch blackness pierced by an immensely powerful beam of light, illuminating this spot of such significance, while the rest of the island, hostile, maleficent, remained cloaked in darkness. Like lights high in the roof of some cosmic theatre, *Nordnorge*'s searchlight beamed down upon this tiny stage whereon was acted out part of one of the most intense dramas of human endeavour. And it all really happened. Right where we were. Right where I was.

ORION IS UPSIDE DOWN

I wrote in my diary that night:

It's a very eerie place, looming up as it did out of the mist and twilight... The open ocean holds no landmarks. GPS is all fine and well, but when you see the island taking form in front of you, you know exactly where you are, and you know exactly what happened right where you are and I realise that maybe sacred ground does exist.

Twenty-eight men in three open boats. Among them, an able-bodied seaman who had grown up looking out from the same shores to the same horizon, wandered the same streets and hung about the same harbour as I had. The world, as I was continuing to discover, is so incredibly vast as to be almost beyond comprehension, yet at the same time so very, very small.

Interlude

Coal is a dirty diamond.

It is 90% carbon, with 'impurities.' Oxygen, nitrogen, sulphur.

Diamonds are 100% carbon. And they say they have no value except that which is placed on them.

The 'impurities' in the would-be diamond make it useful.

Coal is the labourer. Diamond is the aristocrat.

Diamond has the value placed upon it by those who would be like diamond. Coal, the value that those who would be like *coal*.

Put the diamond to work. Make drill bits and surgeons' blades from it. But now we cannot see it, cannot see its beauty and it is its beauty which seduces. But it is the hardest substance known on earth.

To the Greeks it was 'Adamas,' the ancients naming it as we name the adamantium of our speculations about the future.

Hard, like the icebergs. They are diamonds on the ocean, sparkling, beautiful. Deadly.

The coal nourishes. Men feed the machines and they burn it, digest it, turn it into energy; they *move*. They become as living things.

I keep it round my neck.

And it is more valuable than the purest offering of South Africa's richest mines.

It once belonged to *her*, you see. And it is no silly gemstone, no piece of jewellery, utterly useless except as a symbol of excessive wealth, which can buy nothing in the shadow of the Great Leveller. It is the *real* Heart of the Ocean.

People sometimes ask me what it is and seem rather bemused when I reply, 'Coal.' I think they expect it to be obsidian or black onyx or something infused with some sort of preternatural pagan power.

Sodium Potassium Aluminium Silicate - (Na)KAlSi3O8 - is said to protect travellers on the sea. Sounds more transcendental when they call Moonstone.

There is no magic in gemstones, no matter how beautiful, no protective power. They are merely a product of the geological forces of the planet. Just like coal.

My dirty diamond.

CHAPTER 8
The Superhighway of the Sea

I awoke to 360° of grey.

The mist of the sullen Southern Ocean smudged the horizon, leaving no clear divide between sea and sky, just a transition from light to dark in roughly the place where one element should end and the other begin.

I shivered. I had nipped out to take stock of our surroundings only to discover that there weren't any before going for breakfast, and this was not weather to be out in in shirtsleeves. I hoped there would be bacon and eggs. I wanted something hot. As I peered out into the dizzying expanse, a ghost sailed out of the mist, little *James Caird*, *Endurance*'s cutter, rising and falling, rising and falling on the swell that threatened to drown her and her crew with each peak and trough.

Dulwich College.

Dad's had to make special arrangements for this, because of course you can't just go wandering into the hall of a school, not even the school Shackleton went to. It reminds me of the hall in my own secondary, affectionately or otherwise known as the Crush Hall because it got so crowded, usually when the pupils were sheltering from the rain during intervals or lunch breaks.

That which we have come to see is settled behind a railing, mast erect and wearing canvas, but it is furled.

Little James Caird.

And she is little. 23 feet from stem to stern.

A group of boys pours into the hall, they've all just got out of class, released by a bell we'd heard ringing in the distance some moments ago. They drop their bags against the wall - they could have been anyone I'd been in school with - some of them pulling out packets of squashed sandwiches before doing so. I glance at my watch. It's lunchtime. One of them hops up onto the railing and perches there, munching his sandwich. Some sit on the kerb that surrounds the rectangle of shingle the cutter is resting on. Others just stand around. Teenage boys are the same anywhere.

Do they take it for granted, I wonder, that they're hanging around here, eating their lunch next to such a special little ship? Is she just a part of their day-to-day lives, an exhibit in their school? I wonder if they think Dad and I are daft, obviously there for no reason other than to see the ship, with our heavy-duty photographic equipment.

The boys at last pick up their abused bags and shuffle off.

I step up to the bow of the cutter.

Six men, for seventeen days in this tiny vessel.

I did my duty. *Her voice is so soft, so quiet, I hear it only on the edge of my awareness.* I kept them safe. He led them, but I carried them.

Elephant Island could only offer Shackleton and his men temporary respite. Outside of the whaling grounds, no one would come across the band of castaways by chance. So someone would have to go to fetch help.

Leaving under the care and command of Frank Wild twenty-two of those he had shepherded across ice and water, Shackleton took five with him – Frank Worsely, the Navigator; Tom Crean, who but for the grace of God would have been Scott's fifth man four years earlier; Tim McCarthy, to survive all that these seas could throw at him only to be killed in action in the Great War that they had no idea was still raging; Chippy the Carpenter; John Vincent, the Troublemaker. There was always room for redemption, for atonement, with Shackleton. He was the sort of man who might believe there was hope for every fallen angel in hell. But he would make sure he kept an eye on them.

Nordnorge nodded hypnotically as she lumbered onwards through the heavy swell that dominated outside of the influence of any significant landmass. Here, land might not exist anywhere. And we wouldn't see any again for another two days.

Like six men in a boat ninety years ago, we were on our way to South Georgia.

Communities form on board ship. Human beings are social animals and when congregated together in one place will form societies. The same was true on the vessels of Antarctic exploration. The *South Polar Times* was produced on Scott's *Discovery* (and was edited by Shackleton) and on board *Endurance* variety shows were held.

Nordnorge hadn't been at sea long enough for any of that, but it did demonstrate that some things don't change where the sea and its rhythms and symbiosis with humanity is concerned; there had been a note on one of the notice boards (not the hallowed Newspaper Noticeboard, of course) from a trio looking for a fourth bridge player, and someone else lamenting the loss of a lens cap, had anyone found it? Good luck, on that one mate, I'd thought. Losing your first lens cap is a sort of coming of age as a photographer. I've no idea how many Dad and I have left behind between us in the muddy fields in

81

Cumbria through which the Settle and Carlisle railway runs. But I think the loser of the lens cap was more troubled that he had left a plastic item on the fragile shores of Antarctica and was hoping someone could ease his mind rather than wanting the object returned.

And our ship-board community had in place its education system, lectures given by the guides on their various areas of expertise.

This was the third in Arnau's series on the 'discovery' of Antarctica, although I have a little difficulty understanding how something can be discovered if people are sent out to look for it.

Arnau was a small Spanish man for whom history, pre-history, myth and legend were a passion. He spoke good but heavily accented English, but the fast, Spanish lilting and inflections only made his enthusiasm that much more infectious.

Unfortunately during the previous two instalments, a trio of middle-aged American women had decided to correct every mispronounced word (this from a people who pronounce 't' in the middle of a word as 'd' – and I have seen 'water' phonetically presented as *wah' der* in an American dictionary) and every not-quite-right word. But there is a difference between mountain sickness and altitude sickness, and Arnau was *right*. One way to make yourself look really stupid (that's *stew*-pid): 'correct' someone (who's correct anyway) with a wrong technical (or in this case medical) term, so that it's quite obvious you don't actually know what it means. And you look even stupider when the room is full of people who do. It was this that made me realise that there were two camps on board the ship. There were the demographic I now think of as cruise bunnies; the tourists, for whom Antarctica was a prize, a 'When I was in...' name-dropping trophy. And there were the rest of us, who were actually interested in where we were *before* we got here.

Rant over.

I smiled hello to the woman next to me. Hovering around fifty, and with the sort of face that could calm any screaming 2-year-old, she was appropriately dressed, wearing a T-shirt with a large print of Scott's *Discovery* on the front.

I settled down to listen to the lecture. I often wonder how Cook managed to sail right around Antarctica and not catch sight of it once.

* * *

From: webmaster@bbc.co.uk On Behalf of Jack Kernahan
Sent: 23 November 2007 09:08
To: Amy Kernahan
Subject: BBC E-mail: Cruise boat sinking off Argentina

Jack Kernahan saw this story on the BBC News website

and thought you should see it.

Message
Another Antarctica nasty?

** Cruise boat sinking off Argentina **
Passengers and crew members are being rescued from a
sinking cruise liner off Argentina's coast.
<http://news.bbc.co.uk/go/em/fr/-
/hi/world/americas/7108835.stm>

The message was waiting for me when I got back to my desk after our daily
morning 'team meeting' in the tea room.   For a moment, *Nordkapp*'s
misadventure off Deception Island rushing to mind, my insides clenched and I
felt physically ill.   Only a small number of 'cruise' ships are actually tough
enough for polar waters.   Chances were high that it was a ship that I knew.   But
if it had been, Dad would have been gentler breaking the news.   I followed the
link and felt the guilty relief.

Her name was *Explorer*.

I didn't know her.

And to say that she was sinking 'off Argentina' is like saying that
Ascension Island is off the coast of Africa.

She was off King George Island where we had visited Arctowski Base
and found the Tourist Information Office.   And the culprit was unsurprising.

She'd hit an iceberg.

The BBC's report had no photographs.   But I had to know what she
looked like.   I thought Dad would like to know too.

From: Amy Kernahan
Sent: 23 November 2007 09:37
To: Jack Kernahan
Subject: RE: BBC E-mail: Cruise boat sinking off
Argentina
Attachment: 071123.jpg

I think this is her.

From: Jack Kernahan
Sent: 23 November 2007 09:57
To: Amy Kernahan
Subject: RE: BBC E-mail: Cruise boat sinking off
Argentina
Attachment: 060523.jpeg

ORION IS UPSIDE DOWN

```
Think you might be right.
Seem to be quite a few Explorers.
I photographed that Explorer off Armadale in Skye
last May.  I think Waverley might also be in the
photo.
```

So neither of us knew her, but Dad had seen her, further demonstrating that these ships, among them of course *Nordnorge* herself, turn up in the most unexpected places. Armadale? And now she was sinking in the Antarctic.

Good grief, I thought. I was following the events impotently as they happened on the other side of the world. How utterly different from that long ago April, when some reports had *Titanic* still afloat and all safe right until *Carpathia* arrived in New York with only 705 of those 2228 souls aboard.

For me *Titanic* had always been a wreck. I had never actually contemplated witnessing a ship that I had sailed on, that I loved, going through that... transition. I didn't know *Explorer*. Had never sailed on her, had never even seen her. The thought of it being a ship that I knew chilled me to the core, slashed *my* hull.

The Zeebrugge ferry disaster of 1987 got to me. The Ferry Aid single was the first record I ever bought. I recently visited Zeebrugge on board the *QE2*. There's something about that place. A maritime Culloden. The new *Queen Victoria* was there, and despite the 'my horn's better than your horn' shouting match between the ships (which *Elizabeth* won beyond all possibility of doubt) and the general joy at the meeting, as *Victoria* steamed away first there was definitely a sense of Auntie Lizzy watching her with concern.

Be careful, Bairn. Even harbours aren't safe.

And if harbours aren't safe, what then of the untamed and untameable coast of the remotest part of the world?

```
From: Amy Kernahan
Sent: 23 November 2007 12:00
To: Jack Kernahan
Subject: RE: BBC E-mail: Cruise boat sinking off
Argentia
```

```
Nordnorge to the rescue again!
http://news.bbc.co.uk/1/hi/world/americas/7108835.stm
```

I had been watching the BBC updates all morning and now here was the report that rescue ships were on the way, one of them none other than our dear *Nordnorge*. Again. Atta girl, I'd thought proudly, but a little sadly as she became a southern *Carpathia* and took her place among the Antarctic Heroes.

ORION IS UPSIDE DOWN

From: Jack Kernahan
Sent: 23 November 2007 12:28
To Amy Kernahan
Subject: RE: BBC E-mail: Cruise boat sinking off Argentina

Is Nordnorge involved? She seems to be at sea at the moment, but near Antarctic land.
Fram is alongside at Ushuaia.

All the Hurtigrute ships carry webcams on their bridges and a favourite lunchtime diversion for both of us is to 'see what the ships are up to.' Sometimes these webcams can take really good photographs. A friend of ours was once caught by the webcam onboard *Lofoten* (OVDS's 'grand old lady,' built it 1964) and her image was beamed out over the Internet for the next twenty minutes.

I had only the same sources of information Dad had and so I couldn't shed any light on his query.

But I knew someone who probably could.

Message Received: Nov 23 2007, 01:09 PM
From: Amy Kernahan
To: Cecilia Taylor
CC: Jack Kernahan
Subject: Explorer sinking off King George Island.

Hi Cecilia,
http://news.bbc.co.uk/1/hi/world/americas/108835.stm
I've been following some unfolding drama in the Antarctic this morning. M/S Explorer was holed by ice at about 5:30 this morning, has been completely evacuated (which suggests they're going to let her go) and the passengers and crew transferred to other ships, one of which is reported by the BBC to be our Nordnorge. There doesn't seem to be any evidence of the rescue on the webcams at the moment. Could you check your archive to see if it was picked up at all. Of course it's possible that she's still on her way and hasn't picked them up yet.

No human injuries or loss of life.
Cheers

ORION IS UPSIDE DOWN

Amy

Cecilia was the kindly-faced woman I had found myself sitting next to during Arnau's third lecture. Her enthusiasm for the Hurtigrute was enough to make you see stars and her knowledge encyclopaedic. And possibly bordering on obsessive.

And it was Cecilia who took the photograph of Dad that he was so sure was of me.

Her husband, David (who was to later surprise me by appearing in the control room where I was conducting system tests on a satellite), is in software, and is involved with AmSat, the Radio Amateur Satellite Corporation, which holds its annual UK convention at the Surrey Space Centre where I work. What a vast, small world.

Rather than check the Hurtigrute ships' webcams manually and hope for something interesting, as Dad and I do, David has a program that downloads each image broadcast by each webcam (remember, there are eleven ships on the Hurtigrute) which Cecilia later reviews at her leisure and decides which to keep. Personally, I like the lucky feeling of stumbling upon a good image, and knowing that what ever is depicted happened within the last twenty minutes. That's just me. But now it was about to be seen that apparently obsessive behaviour can have its uses, so never be afraid to be a little insane!

From: Cecilia Taylor
Sent: 23 November 2007 12:36
To: Amy Kernahan
CC: Jack Kernahan
Subject: RE: Explorer sinking off King George Island
Attachments: 2007-11-23-1102-f.jpg; 2007-11-23-117-f.jpg; 2007-11-23-1132-s.jpg

Yes Amy, I just got in having had the collection of Nordnorge webcam photos activated, and found the three views of Explorer, attached.

Latest reports indicate that everyone has been picked up by NN and will be landed at King George Island from where there is a possibility of being flown out. It looks as if NN is already just off land, but the previously good weather has apparently become windier and they are reported as intending to wait a while before landing anyone.

Below is the url to an interview with our Captain

ORION IS UPSIDE DOWN

Arnvid Hansen. I'm sure you will enjoy hearing his
lovely Norwegian accent again.

http://news.bbc.co.uk/player/nol/newsid_7100000/newsi
d_7109400/7109402.stm

Cheers, Cecilia

The final resting place of MV *Explorer* is 62° 24'17.57" South, 57° 11'46.49"
West.

Cecilia was the first person I'd ever met (apart from my dad) who understood.
    After getting chatting after that lecture we went to the 'Veranda Café'
(Dad had nicknamed it after the approximate equivalent on *Titanic* and I had
approved, wishing that I'd thought of it) for coffee and we must have talked for
about two hours. (Dad eventually found us, and suggested lunch might be a
good idea before the hungry hordes devoured the lot.)
    I listened to the way she talked about the ships, the tone of voice, the
anthropomorphic language she used…
    We started talking about *Titanic*.
I have a secret. It is what makes me different from thousands of others. It is
what makes me special.
    I trusted this woman.
    I decided to tell her.
    'I've touched her,' I said. '*Titanic*.'

*The room is dim and cool, a single soft spotlight on its only occupant, the
photons dancing over her surface, and she appears to be the source of the light.
Decades under water have ensured that she will never fully regain her former
lustre, but the loss is dignified, like graceful old age. She is not behind glass,
but is suspended in eternity from a ceiling lost in darkness. Only a low railing
on the floor below, circular, no more than twelve inches high, prevents too close
an approach. I am breathing air that has wrapped itself around that tarnished
brass which is more precious than gold, and that air will glide across it again
after I exhale. In the pale, watery light and surrounding gloom I wonder if she
realises that she is no longer on the bottom of the ocean.*
    *They did right. They found her in the debris field. What are the chances
of finding a single seventeen-inch diameter bell in the several square miles of
seabed littered with objects that tumbled out as the ship fell? However one may
feel about salvage, in this one instance, they did right.*
    *She is alone, and I am alone, 3,000 miles from home, in a city where
among hundreds of other conference delegates, I am nothing more than my
profession.*

I know who you are.

The tears are streaming now, warm salt water as my offering to warm the cold in which her broken body lies.

We meet at last. At last. At last. At last.

And I cannot leave her.

In the deep there is no time, no sun or moon or stars to mark its passing.

'Are you all right?'

'All my life.' My voice is barely audible but the effort makes it feel like I am shouting. 'All my life. I can hardly remember a time before her.'

The woman next to me is not much taller than I am. She's wearing a long dress that touches the floor and a bustle. She stands by me, puts an arm around my shoulders. But human warmth and skin and softness are not what I want or need. The woman recognises that.

'You can touch her.'

My whispered 'Thank you' is accepted with a smile from strangely knowing eyes. I step over the non-barrier and touch the rim of that beautiful bell with the fingers of both hands, my warm, soft skin sliding briefly over the cold, hard brass in the caress that I have longed to give and receive since I was six years old.

'I love you.'

The woman in the bustle wraps her arms around me as I step from the pool of light that bathes the ship's soul back in to the darkness and I sob into the hollow between her shoulder and neck.

'Let me take you to the surface.'

As I take one last look around that simple mausoleum, I hear the music.

Time begins again.

I have been there three hours.

No, I hadn't seen a ghost, or gone mad. The woman in the bustle had been one of a number of museum staff in period dress. But the music... At first I thought it was 'Nearer My God To Thee,' but although similar in parts it was clearly a different tune. I found out months later that it was the Songe d'Automne. To the best of my knowledge, I had never heard it before that afternoon in the Houston Museum of Natural History.

CHAPTER 9
Sovereign Powers are not Penguins

I felt rather foolish afterwards. Felt very foolish for having convinced my dad to come along. I was sure he was unlikely to let me forget it in a hurry. But I must take full responsibility for our attendance at a lecture on penguins.

As if there weren't enough of the silly creatures toddling around tripping us up every time we set foot ashore, I had to go and volunteer us to listen to someone talk about them for an hour while we were at sea.

In my defence I can only say that I misunderstood the title of the lecture. It was 'The Kings of South Georgia.' I knew who George III ('Georgia') was, and I assumed the Edward of King Edward Point was Edward VII, but I wanted to know who King Haakon and Prince Olaf might have been. I should have twigged immediately when the lecturer, Spherical Penguin Lady, who's real name was Brigette, arrived in the forward bar. But it was only when she turned around to face her audience and took her place by the lectern that I realised my grave error.

'Er, Da-a-a-d,' I said, feeling my ears growing warm. 'I think I've made a mistake.'

'Oh?'

'It's all over her T-shirt.'

And so it was.

'South Georgia' was printed across the chest, forming a banner over the regal image of... a king penguin. Oops. We were not really in a position to easily extricate ourselves, so we shuffled a little in our seats, suddenly aware that we were surrounded by penguin enthusiasts who probably now thought we were too. I hoped none of them would try to start a conversation with me about Macaronis in the lunch queue.

Penguins are fascinating!

They're not confined to the extreme high latitudes. They even wander across the equator on occasions. And they're *hard*. Apsely Cherry-Garrard was right when he said 'No one has a worse time than the emperor penguin.' They just stand there. On the ice shelf. All winter. I want to introduce a new simile to the English language – tough as a penguin.

And there are gay penguins. The behaviour has been observed in a very tiny species called... oh dear.

I wasn't going to say anything. I *wasn't* going to say *anything*. But next to me Dad was pinching the bridge of his nose with his eyes screwed up.

'Do you think that's why they're called fairy penguins?' he asked, his voice almost completely smothered by the effort not to laugh.

My own politically incorrect sniggers escaped then and that was it. All attempts at taking the subject seriously were abandoned to the (allegedly) Force

9 wind and we sat there for the remainder of the lecture nudging each other and giggling and looking for every opportunity to take the mickey like a pair of naughty schoolchildren.

There are no fairy penguins in Antarctica.

The ship was still nodding quite enthusiastically. During dinner, which was a *kalt bord* and so everyone was wandering around the restaurant collecting their food then negotiating their way back to their tables, it had begun to seem possible that the weather display on the screen by the courier's desk might not have been exaggerating with its report of 'Force 9.' On such occasions it was fun to observe how many passengers had found their sea legs… and also how many hadn't. What I had not expected to see was someone skidding past me holding on to his plate with both hands and trying to keep an eye on his feet, muttering to no obvious listener, 'This is worse than the Minch.'

The Minch is the stretch of sea that separates the Outer Hebrides from mainland Scotland.

I don't know if I'd have been more surprised if a white rabbit had hurried past, declaring that it was late.

I turned to Dad, who was quite comfortably carrying a bowl of soup and a bread roll in one hand.

'Was he talking to you?'

'Who?'

'A bloke just went tottering off in that direction' – I pointed – 'saying "This is worse than the Minch."'

Dad looked puzzled.

'It's not, though,' he said.

I took a wander on deck after the evening's movie. I was hoping for clear skies. Clouds congregate around landmasses, a behaviour of weather I have been aware of all my life, living on a landmass (if Lewis can be called a 'mass') right on the edge of the North Atlantic. An entire ocean's worth of cloud tends to congregate over that little island. I had been hoping that now that we were at sea, twenty four hours away from our last sight of land, that I might get to see stars that I'd never seen before.

The stars are constant. So constant that mariners have been using them as guides for centuries. No matter where they were in the world, the stars would always be there, something familiar, and could always lead them home. A place that was so far away that those stars were not visible and others had taken their place was like a sailor's tale, along with mermaids and sea monsters and falling off the edge. And yet, the reality existed. And I was here, in that far-away place. Where even the stars are different.

But the weather was not going to oblige me. Standing at the bow, away from the ship's running lights, the sky and the ocean met in an unbroken black veil into which *Nordnorge* steamed steadily on.

Spray flew up with each wave she rode, showering her forecastle with phosphorescence. I turned my back on the darkness and went indoors to the lights and the warmth and the chatter in several different languages.

And there on *Nordnorge*'s forecastle lay that massive black anchor, unnoticed by the scores of passengers who stood at the bow each day.

Not long now.

There is a difference between knowledge and belief.

I was woken by Something making a noise straight out of my nightmares against the outside wall of my cabin. I *knew* it couldn't possibly be what it sounded like, I just didn't *believe* it.

It had haunted my more malevolent dreams since I was seven years old, since I started seeing a White Star cabin around me in the no man's land between waking and sleeping.

(I know where the term 'stateroom' comes from, and as a result I refuse to use it. The more opulent cabins on American riverboats were named after American states, and the use of the term carried across to ocean liners. I'm sure this is some sort of nautical racism, but I don't *do* American riverboats. Nothing that hideous should to be afloat.)

I had heard the sound once before. In my cabin aboard the little icebreaker *Polar Star*, low down, near the waterline. I knew what ice scraping the hull of a ship sounds like.

The knowledge that this was *Nordnorge*, and my cabin was high in the superstructure with a promenade deck running by its outside wall, and that we were now far too far north and that no ice had come within miles and miles of us for two days was swamped by fear.

If I open that blind and find we're in an ice-field...

Of course we weren't. *Nordnorge* was being given a bath, and it was the hoses against the outer wall of my cabin that had catapulted me into a pagophobic panic.

CHAPTER 10
A Tale of a Tail of a Whale

'I see Brigette's repeating her lecture in German this morning,' I said over breakfast. I wasn't going to say anything about my wake-up call.

'You don't fancy going?'

'Not particularly, no.'

'How is your German, by the way?'

'Embryonic.'

'Aborted' would probably have been nearer the truth. I'd been making a valiant effort about a year previously and on my way to a job interview in Darmstad I had succeeded in purchasing my rail ticket at Frankfurt Hauptbahnhof with the entire verbal exchange carried out in German. This gestated in me the mistaken belief that I could actually speak the language. A couple of hours later in the hotel, all that the receptionist understood of my apology for speaking German not so good and enquiry as to whether she spoke English was 'englisch.' I thanked the divine power which watches over me that the official languages of the interviewing agency were English and French, both of which I can muddle through in. I didn't get the job. Glad I didn't. I doubt if anyone outside the 'space community' whatever that is – loose confederation of warring tribes would be more accurate, my thanks to *Yes, Minister* for the analogy – has ever heard of Venus Express. The similarity between the project and my German is remarkable.

'What's the English lecture?'

'Something about whales and dolphins,' I replied, reading it off the day's schedule. '"A Whale of a Tale" it's called.'

'Not "A Tail of a Whale"?'

I resisted the temptation to flick a forkful of omelette at him; Francisco, our waiter, was hovering in the vicinity.

We hadn't seen so much as a tail of a whale. Apart from some enormous vertebrae lying on the beach at Arctowski, this lecture would be the closest we'd come to one. Whales seemed to be in inverse proportion to penguins, with zero of the former corresponding to infinity of the latter.

Instead of starting a food fight, I turned to matters domestic.

'We need to do a laundry.'

'We can do that this afternoon, then.'

I was momentarily reminded of working night-shift at thermal vacuum testing. I would hold off on documentation that I would normally want to get out of the way immediately in order to give me something to do at three o'clock in the morning.

Dad was now examining the schedule. It really ought to have been a newspaper he peered over as he answered, but they were pinned to the wall in the library and no-one was privileged enough to have their own copy.

Congregating around the newspapers was one of the social events of village life on board the ship. No matter when you went, there would always be at least three of your fellow countrymen there, although this was obviously not the case for Terry, who was the only Irishman on board. I wasn't quite sure what to make of the presence of the newspapers. Here we were, about as far from civilisation as it was possible to get, bobbing around in a big steel container (sorry, *Nordnorge*) and we could still see what the Dow Jones or Footsie were doing. Or be depressed by the football results. Maybe I was still a little annoyed by the loss to Southampton and was blaming the bearer of the bad news. Perhaps there are no great wildernesses anymore. For all it's making the world safer – the debate is on-going even almost a hundred years later as to what *Titanic*'s last position on the surface actually was – technology has made it smaller. I thought of Shackleton, at the end of his epic journey, asking the governor of the Stromness whaling station when the war, newly declared when *Endurance* had set out, had ended, only to be told that it was raging still and the carnage was beyond anything anyone could have imagined. Perhaps they were better off not knowing. Had they known what sort of a world they were coming back to, would the will to survive have been quite so strong? And it made me think of James Cameron, on one of his later dives to the *Titanic* wreck site, setting off in a MIR submersible one September morning in 2001. He returned to the news that the Twin Towers had collapsed in the greatest terrorist attack the world had ever known. While he was on the bottom of the ocean. Perhaps that's the closest modern equivalent of the men of the Imperial Trans-Antarctic Expedition's severance from the world. And it made me think of the days following *Titanic*'s sinking, the conflicting reports relayed by wireless, so primitive to us now but one of the new technological marvels of the Edwardian age. We take for granted our as-it-happens, satellite-relayed news bulletins, and we complain if our broadband isn't *quite* fast enough. How would we manage, sitting in a hut made from an upturned boat for four months... waiting. Waiting for the man to whom we still entrusted our lives even though he had just left us and sailed out into that vast emptiness. Waiting for him to return.

This was our second day of open ocean. Our second day surrounded by nothing. If it was daunting and awe-inspiring to me, safely cradled in this strong working ship, what must it have been like for Shackleton and his five-man crew in their tiny open boat? But when every moment is concentrated on living to see the next, one can't have time to think. The technology that gives us the blessing of safety also gives us the curse of time. Time to contemplate that vastness and to think upon and conjure up dangers and monsters which would not have troubled those six men; they simply didn't have time to acknowledge their existence.

Visibility, if it can be called that when there is nothing to see, was an improvement on yesterday. The line between the sea and sky was sharp, as though drawn with a pair of compasses, the focus in the middle of *Nordnorge*'s upper deck, where I was now, becoming part of the deck fixtures, had there been anyone else who spent enough time here to notice. Up here, out here, you *rode* the ship. Her movement, a steady pitching as she dipped her prow into each oncoming swell, which showered over her forecastle as she rose, was pronounced, with only the horizon as a reference to her rise and fall. And of course, the human inner ear.

Each day on the schedule along with lecture times and landing times (as appropriate) was the word of the day in English, Norwegian and German. Today's was 'seasick' (*Sjosyk, Seekrank*). I had noticed quite a number of passengers wandering around with little flesh-coloured patches about the size of a penny (or Euro-cent) behind their ears. I'd been curious about them, and the realisation had hit me like a eureka moment.

'They're to prevent seasickness!'

Dad had looked at me as though my inherent madness (inherited from him) had crept up a notch.

'What are?'

We had been people-watching in the corridor lounge on Deck 4, amazed that the queue to get into the restaurant for lunch, which opened at twelve o'clock, started to form around eleven thirty.

'Those little patches behind people's ears. They must be acting directly on the little tubes and things that affect your balance.'

Little tubes and things. Such is the extent of my mastery of medical vocabulary.

Having realised what they were for, I began mischievously to look out for them ('Hee-hee! Andreas has got seasick!'), but noted with pride that none of the British contingent were sporting any. Here, at least, we were proving that we were a race of mariners.

Now, out on the top deck, I decided to film a full sweep of the empty horizon, as I could see it, and indeed, it was all there was to see. The ship chose *that* moment, when I had twisted at the waist to a degree that I'm sure you're not supposed to after the age of about fifteen, to drop suddenly, breaking the steady rhythm I had tuned myself into.

Ha-ha! Caught you out!

Being born of a 'race of mariners' will not stop ships trying occasionally to throw you to the deck. But they're only playing.

I didn't quite fall over. Usually I felt quite sad that the majority of passengers stayed huddled away inside – even though perhaps a little selfishly I liked having the deck to myself, they just didn't know what they were missing – but right now I was glad there was no-one there to witness *Nordnorge* 'playing' with me.

There was nothing out there. And at the same time there was so much out there. So much to see, so much to learn. The human lifespan was, to me, suddenly woefully inadequate. 'Three score years and ten,' although now extended by medical advances, was nowhere near enough. This was the true consequence of the Fall, that we should be taken out of this amazing world before we have seen even a fraction of its wonders.

We decided to do the laundry after the briefing for our South Georgia landings. It would be something to do for the hour before dinner, that strange limbo time between five and six o'clock when I always feel I ought to be doing something. The laundry room would be quiet then – most of the passengers would be standing outside the restaurant.

The little laundry room was on Deck 2.

F-Deck, the sea dog in me growled.

Or maybe it would be G-deck. I wasn't sure if under the 'traditional' naming convention what we called Deck 8 would be the Boat Deck, as there were no boats on it. They were suspended above Deck 5, offering ineffective shelter from the wind, rain, spray and anything else the ocean decided to throw at us. Like a flock of tiny birds.

It happened one night, after we'd left the Falklands. Dozens of miniature kamikazes hurled themselves out of the darkness at the ship's superstructure. They weren't very successful kamikazes, as they caused no damage to the ship and minimal damage to themselves, but Manuel, the expedition ornithologist, did go out on deck and gathered a few of the poor dazed little creatures under his jacket and stroked the soft feathers on their spinning heads until they were sufficiently recovered to fly off again into the darkness from whence they came, their brief moment in the light consisting of a collision with a monstrous object and the consequent pain and disorientation.

Was it any different in the end for those little birds that picked themselves up off the deck and flew away back into the night than it was for those Manuel picked up and cuddled? For the former there was blinding light and pain, but they recovered and went on their way as before. For the latter there was blinding light and pain, but some great being had held them until the pain stopped, and then they went on their way as before; he didn't try to stop them. Maybe those little birds would believe that there was something 'more,' a protective presence that the others, having not experienced it, would not understand, would not 'believe in,' even though in the end it ultimately made no difference. To those little birds would Manuel be God?

For all my frustration with changes to maritime terminology, I am grateful that 'port' and 'starboard' still have their rightful place. One of my favourite moments from the movie *Master and Commander* is when Babbington has to refer to a sailor's right arm as his 'starboard arm' to get him to understand what he means. Before we had made it to the purser's office to get the little tokens needed to operate the washing machine the intercom chimed and the courier announced that a whale had been spotted off the port bow.

Those passengers not standing in the queue for the restaurant, or those who were willing to sacrifice their place in it, spilled out on deck after various detours for photographic equipment.

Here was an instance where my Dad's inside-out knowledge of these ships and careful planning gave us an advantage.

Dad had specifically requested cabins 520 and 521, which were right next to the main door onto Deck 5, the promenade deck that ran right around the perimeter of the superstructure. On our way to the main pedestrian artery of the ship we would always pass our cabins, thus collecting cameras would not cause appreciable delays.

While others were hurrying off into the higher superstructure or down into the bowels of the ship we were taking our places at the bow unobstructed. The whale didn't seem to be in too much of a hurry to leave us, so the camera-scramblers weren't disappointed, but when you're five-foot-three getting near the front becomes quite important. And people don't tend to resent it because they can just point their camera right over your head.

So Dad got his Tail of a Whale after all.

But that wasn't the only prophecy from that morning to be fulfilled.

In the distance an angular white shape disturbed the horizon. It was difficult to see, but…

It's just there, separating sea from sky, the first feature to mar the horizon since we left Elephant Island, diffusing into the mist ahead, ephemeral, evanescent; but there are few substances on the planet that are more solid. It is a massive chunk of a glacier, a glacier old enough to leave home. It has outgrown the land and stretched out into the sea and finally detached. The ice that forms it, those ancient snowfalls from time before memory, has already scraped away the surface of the Antarctic bedrock on its way to the ocean. The berg is vast, and the seascape is one that would not be unexpected in poor visibility when approaching the southeast coast of England. But the White Cliffs of Dover, soft chalk and limestone, would be no match for it. It has ripped away far harder rock than that, and the fjords of Norway and the mountains of Scotland bear witness to that. It is no wonder that the first southern explorers mapped these frozen leviathans as islands on charts, and so added to the mysteries of *Terra Australis Incognita* – islands that simply disappeared.

And disappearing they are.

We hear about it every other week or so.

Climate change.

Global Warming.

The ice caps are melting.

But it will not go without a fight. It is constantly on the offensive, advancing in winter as the sea freezes and sending out its lone assassins in spring as the warmer weather, warmer than it has been in millions of years if you believe all you read, allows icebergs the size of entire counties and larger to break away. And after they do so, they will not return. They leave in order to die, be that a natural death as they have met in centuries gone by, simply to drift into warmer waters, or one accelerated by changing global temperatures.

The berg charges north, as if perhaps to exert some kind of revenge upon the human creatures that are slowly, if unintentionally, killing it the only way it can if they do not come to it but it must go to them – by attacking them and the steel containers they must reside in if they are to survive in this element which the bergs so easily inhabit.

The early months of 1912 had been abnormally warm in the high northern latitudes and the ice had drifted unusually far south. And entered the shipping lanes. Of course, there is no reasonable way one can blame planes, trains and automobiles for that. Not at that point in the industrialisation of the western world. But right now, it continues to stretch on along the horizon to port, both ends now hidden in the mist. This is it, the ocean of the high latitudes, north or south, the ocean of my blood and soul, and the ice is its natural master.

The Angel of
God took me, and he of Hell cried out, "O thou from Heaven, why
dost thou rob me? Thou bearest away for thyself the eternal
part of him for one little tear which takes him from me; but of
the rest I will make other disposal."[xl]

It has taken something special and precious. But like Shackleton, I conquer by continuing.
Yes, she is lost, but I still imagine that she will be there, on that Glassy Sea, before the throne of the Ancient of Days, the 'eternal part' 'born away,' leaving the demon to do as it would with what was left, now lying twisted and broken on the bottom of the Atlantic Ocean.

I loathe it so much I love it, and I watching it here on the ocean, where it is the natural if cold and cruel lord, I mourn for the ice caps as they recede further and further each year.

I do not want it to die.

No matter what it has done, it does not deserve extinction.

It is a tabular berg, not a mountain of ice but a great slab of the ice sheet, severed from the parent glacier. We were far north of the territory of the pack, but here was a lone monster on the prowl. Separated from the collective, it was diminished but not weakened. One would be a fool to believe it any less deadly.

Stay away.

Nordnorge did.

Maybe my morning terror hadn't been quite so irrational after all. Maybe a part of me had known that we weren't out of the ice's realm yet, that to drop guard now would be to invite danger. After all, we hadn't even reached South Georgia, an island whose interior is held in the ice's eternal grip. No one would deny its sovereignty there.

We didn't get the laundry done.

Interlude

"Get on your knees and pray for Shackleton."

In such circumstances, 'when disaster strikes and no hope is left,' just what is one praying for when one invokes the name of Shackleton?

Inspiration to find a way out of an impossible situation?

Strength of will and body to go on when all seems hopeless?

The charisma to keep those with you from despair?

Or the courage to keep pressing on into an unknown that harbours pain and hardship and the probability of death?

Yes, all that. And a different kind of courage: the courage to fail.

'Yes, sir, we failed. We failed to reach the South Pole. I chose life over death for myself and my men…'

He was speaking about the 1907 *Nimrod* expedition, an endeavour surrounded by controversies and alleged breaches of honour.

The 1901 *Discovery* expedition with Captain Scott in command, of course did not succeed in reaching the South Pole, and there is a common belief that Scott held Shackleton, who had fallen ill with scurvy, to blame.

I have read Scott's own account of the expedition, and I see no such matter. Shackleton did not start showing signs of disease or weakness until they were on their way back, having already abandoned the pursuit of the Pole. Indeed, in his book Scott praises Shackleton highly. The rivalry advocates will claim that this is nothing more than good Edwardian Britishness, that to speak well, indeed exaggeratedly so, of another man no matter how you really felt about him was considered the only behaviour appropriate for a gentleman. Or it might have been true.

I looked a little deeper into it. The origins of the myth clearly did not lie with Scott.

They lay with the *Daily Mail*.

If you can bear to see the truth you've spoken
Twisted by knaves to make a trap for fools…

Mountains erode and are washed to the sea, deserts advance and retreat, continents grind together and pull apart opening new oceans, but there are things in this world which do not change.

Only the names. O Prophetic soul…

So Shackleton's culpability in Scott's eyes, for the failure of the *Discovery* expedition appears to have been what one may euphemistically call a misunderstanding, but the bitterness Scott certainly felt towards his former comrade does not. So what changed?

This time, it was the *Times*, which reported that the 'main objective' of Shackleton's planned expedition (the 1907 *Nimrod* expedition) was 'to follow the discoveries made on the southern sledge journey from the *Discovery*,' having landed the shore party in McMurdo Sound, the same landing point as had been used in 1901.

While it was true that at that time Shackleton did intend to use that landing point, the newspaper implied that Shackleton intended to succeed where 'Scott' had failed, using the ground-work laid by 'Scott' to do so.

But why shouldn't he? He had been as much a member of that expedition as Scott himself was, even if the naval crew considered him a 'passenger,' especially, and ironically, when it came to handling the ship; his years spent aboard the *Houghton Tower* meant that he had far better experience of sail than anyone else on board, even if he did think *Discovery* was a poor sailer.

Shackleton, after receiving an emotional letter from Scott (the first communication between the two for four years), promised that he would not land in McMurdo Sound.

It was a promise he did not keep, but not by design. The alternative anchorage he had intended to use, the expedition discovered upon arrival, no longer existed. It had been at the snout of a glacier which had calved, taking the bay that had once been there with it. No safe haven was to be found within the area from which Scott had excluded Shackleton and so much time was spent searching that little *Nimrod* would have been in danger of running out of coal before she could return to New Zealand if they continued their futile hunt any longer. The original Nimrod may have been 'a mighty hunter before the Lord' but that did not extend to his namesake finding a safe anchorage where the very nature of the land and sea meant that it was constantly changing. Indeed, it is likely that had Shackleton not made the decision to make for McMurdo Sound, *Nimrod*'s captain, Rupert England, would have done it anyway.

The laws of the sea are incontrovertible: on board a ship, her captain's word is absolute and Shackleton, although fully qualified, was not the captain of his ship. Another rule equally inviolable is that the plight of a ship in distress must not go unanswered, even during times of war. A victorious attacking ship must pick up survivors from the vanquished. This extends to granting of safe passage and anchorage. For one seaman to deny another safe haven is, in the mind of any mariner, far more heinous than the breaking of a 'gentleman's agreement.' And in these circumstances that was what Scott, with his demand that Shackleton stay away from McMurdo Sound, was doing. The laws of the sea are ancient, far older than any Edwardian concepts of chivalry. Such patterns of behaviour and society come and go, but the sea and men of the sea remain. Shackleton, the Edwardian gentleman, was tortured by the decision that Shackleton, the seaman, had made. He wrote to his wife Emily, 'My conscience is clear but my heart is sore,' and that 'I have been through a sort of Hell.'

Scott never forgave him.

If being hated not give way to hating

Indeed Scott got quite worked up and blew things out of all reasonable proportion. He took this 'breach of promise' as evidence that nothing

Shackleton said could be trusted. To Louis Bernacchi Scott confided, "I am sure he is prepared to lie rather than admit failure."

This from the man who history proved was prepared to *die* rather than admit failure, while Shackleton confessed his.

'It seems hard that we cannot do the remainder,' he wrote on his decision to turn back. 'But as it is absolutely certain we should all die if we did, it would not do us or the world any good.'

If you can see the things you gave your life to broken
And stoop and build 'em up again with worn out tools.

So who was the braver man?

'Better a live donkey than a dead lion,' Shackleton had written to Emily Scott, a dead lion.

Wasn't it prophesied by Isaiah that the Messiah would come riding on a donkey, and don't the Gospels record that He did? Does that not make the humble donkey a truly noble beast?

History refines, and like the constant action of the sea turning jagged rocks into smooth pebbles, removes the sharper points that may injure or draw blood from the national pride. Shackleton is lauded as a heroic failure; what seems to be forgotten is that Scott failed too. He died failing. And ultimately Shackleton achieved more in his failure than most men do in their successes.

If you can meet with Triumph and Disaster
And treat these two impostors just the same…

We are the sum of our choices.

Shackleton chose: the safety of his ship, the lives of his men.

Scott chose: a 'gentleman's agreement' belonging to a transient period in history over the law of the sea, established since man first set sail in his little coracles.

And which is more, you'll be a man, my son.

It made great drama, but I had sought truth.

The insinuation of the article in the *Times* was that the rivalry originated with Shackleton.

If being lied about don't deal in lies

Shackleton was the subject of a blatant lie, albeit an implied one.

Scott suffered the consequences of believing that lie to be true.

While it does not excuse any of his subsequent behaviour, Scott's paranoia was not entirely a product of his own imagination. Perhaps we can forgive him. With no features from which to gain perspective, molehills look like mountains on the Antarctic wastes. Scott even recognised that he was being manipulated. Again he confided to Louis Bernacchi, 'I don't like to be forced into such a false position of apparent jealousy.'

Any rivalry between Scott and Shackleton should never have been, for it was created in Scott by the false report that it existed in Shackleton.

And the common belief that Scott held Shackleton responsible for the failure of the Discovery expedition is the result of the intervention of the *Daily Mail*.

These two men should never have been enemies.

'He who steals my purse steals trash
'Twas something, nothing, 'twas mine, 'tis his
A slave to thousands.
But he who filches from me my good name
Robs me of that which enriches him not
And leaves me poor indeed.'

It was Iago who said that.

Of course, Shakespeare's super-villain has had many faces and voices over the last four hundred years. But I have never heard Ernest Shackleton speak, and the voice I associate with him is one of those that has given utterance to these lines.

Oh, and *Titanic*'s owners never claimed that she was unsinkable.

It was the newspapers. They took a few words in an engineering journal out of context.

CHAPTER 11
Grytviken

'We go to gain a little patch of ground,' said Fortinbras' captain, 'that hath in it no profit but the name. To pay five ducats, five, I would not farm it.'

'Why then the Polack never will defend it,' replied Hamlet.

'Yes. It is already garrisoned.'

'Rightly to be great,' concluded the Danish prince after discussing the issue with himself at some length, 'is not to stir without great argument, but greatly to find quarrel in a straw when honour's at the stake.'

South Georgia was such a straw.

The Falklands Conflict began when an Argentinean scrap merchant landed at Leith (an abandoned whalers' settlement on South Georgia, not the town in Scotland) bringing with him a contingent of Argentine armed forces.

The aggressor's intention seems to have been to first take South Georgia and then use it as a base from which to invade the Falkland Islands. The right of title to the Falkland Islands is a complex issue, but the Islands *do* have an indigenous population descended from British settlers with absolutely no desire to become Argentinean. Argentina seems to have selectively ignored this as they have recently begun sending pregnant women to Antarctica so that Argentinean children will be born there. Thus Antarctic 'natives' will be the offspring of Argentine citizens therefore Antarctica will belong to Argentina. Falkland Island 'natives' are the descendants of British settlers therefore the Falklands belong to...Argentina as well. Insufficient logic. Does not compute.

That great non-hero of my primary school days, Captain Cook, discovered South Georgia too, in 1775. He called it 'savage and horrible.' So I'm not convinced he was ever actually there.

It is the same latitude south as Lewis is north.

Were it not for the Gulf Stream, would the island I grew up on have spent its winters encased in ice? Would the Clisham have been a majestic peak, snow-covered even in summer? Would the Barvas moor have lain permanently beneath a glacier?

Could Lewis have looked like *that*?

But it comes at a price. Those very things that give South Georgia its beauty make it hostile. It beckons, then as suitors approach denies. Cook was wrong. South Georgia is not savage and horrible, it is savage and beautiful, and that is far crueller. Grumpy old Lewis, with its rain, wind, rain, perpetual cloud cover, and rain, mushy peat bogs, feeble attempts at hills, and no trees has grudgingly supported human beings for millennia. Hardly a crucible of civilisation like the Nile delta, and those who made it their home scraped their living along the coast, but scrape it they did.

It's Christmas Eve, five years since my visit to that Lewis-in-the-Southern-Hemisphere. The whole of the UK is ensnared by the coldest winter anyone can remember. I'm with my family for Christmas, although the snow that has recently crippled the transport network has made it an epic journey. But today the sun is shining on the snowfall of the last week or so, and in these high northern latitudes the winter sun is low and strong and calls colours into being with the same splendour as it does in the south. I've taken a long walk around the perimeter of the grounds of Lews Castle and am returning along the Shore Road which runs above the shore of the harbour opposite the town. Looking down to the rocks along the water's edge, I do a double-take. The surface of the water is covered with pancake ice, the discs of sea ice that form in the first stages of the big freeze in the polar regions. I look out across the water, and see seagulls apparently performing miracles. At the pontoons and berths on the opposite shore, fishing boats and yachts are beset.

Stornoway Harbour has iced over.

The ship had received special permission from the South Georgia government to detour to Drygalski Fjord before reporting in at King Edward Point. All ships visiting South Georgia are required to call there for inspection. It was

Constantino Davidoff, the scrap merchant's failure to do this and his subsequent landing of men and equipment at Leith that constituted an invasion in theory. When his ship began disgorging Argentine militia it constituted an invasion in practice. The hoisting of the Argentinean flag on the island might as well have been a declaration of war. But that was to come later.

I was woken by the hoses again at six o'clock and discovered that we were already entering Drygalski Fjord. I had hoped that we would be able to watch South Georgia approach on the horizon as we had Elephant Island, and hauling myself out onto the sunny deck to look around at a fjord that could easily have been in Norway was a little anticlimactic. But the weather was superb, and I forgave my rude awakening (although not the fright it had once again given me) as being out on deck was far preferable to hiding under my blanket in dreams still haunted by immense white monsters.

Running along the coast towards our rendezvous at King Edward Point, no-one seemed happier than *Nordnorge* herself. Restricted to fifteen knots at home in Norway, obliged to keep to the speed of the slower, but by no means less lively, older vessels in the fleet, the youngsters seemed to rejoice when their masters allowed them to gallop.

Absorbed by the island's beauty, I was becoming more indignant with Captain Cook for calling it 'savage and horrible' with each passing minute when Nature decided to improve upon the perfection of the vista before us by adding one of her greatest wonders – a rainbow. A considerable number of the ship's complement came rushing to the port side as the word spread. Rainbows always make me feel like a child again, when I just accepted that the animals all went into the Ark two by two and it didn't matter that it was logistically impossible, and on Lewis we often *did* need assurance that God wouldn't destroy the world with a deluge again. Though I had often wondered why Noah saved wasps. He would have done posterity a great favour if he'd let them all drown. And as I gazed with quiet awe upon the spectacle we were all admiring I felt a small stirring of pride and privilege with the knowledge that only I could see it.

At a summer school I once attended one of the lecturers explained that because of the way in which rainbows are formed, white sunlight separating into its spectrum as it passes through the raindrops, everybody looking at it sees the light passing through different raindrops. Even if you're standing right next to someone, the angle at which you are looking to the place where the light is being split will be slightly different. Therefore you will see the rainbow in a slightly different place. It is your own personal rainbow, and no-one else can see it.

We lay at anchor off King Edward Point while the ship was inspected, and two little boats belonging to the Government of South Georgia Harbour Patrol zipped around us curiously as though they were trying to find out who this (relative) leviathan was who had invaded their harbour and was taking up so much room. I imagined the Magistrate sitting in one of the white buildings on the pier on an April morning in 1982, the master of an Argentinean warship informing him of the fall of Stanley and demanding his surrender. I saw ghostly Argentinean troops charging towards the scientific station, and Royal Marines valiantly defending it for two hours until the enemy started shelling them from offshore. And then, only twenty-two days later, those same Argentinean troops waving a white flag, perhaps a handkerchief or somebody's shirt. The wind that whipped us even at anchor in the sheltered bay carried across the years the booming guns of Her Majesty's Ships *Antrim* and *Plymouth* as they enthusiastically bombarded two positions across the bay, terrifying the occupying forces into surrender. Of course I knew nothing about actual troop movements or what form the Argentinean surrender took. But shades had formed in my imagination that could no longer be confined to black words on white pages of books identified as 'history' even although the events described took place during my lifetime. Not now that I was looking at this place in colours stronger and brighter than ever they appeared under industrial Northern skies.

A couple of hundred metres along the shore from King Edward Point lies Grytviken, frozen in time, but not immune to its whips and scorns. It was the first shore-based whaling station to be established in the Antarctic, and was the last to close[14]. Three whaling boats, *Petrel*, *Albatross* and *Dias* lie at their moorings just as they were left when the station was abandoned, like three little *Mary Celeste*s. They wait patiently for their masters to come back to them. They never will.

Unperturbed by the visitor in the bay, JCBs trundled around between the buildings of the community that had once existed there. The clean-up operation is under way, to make Grytviken safe. Imbued with toxic substances and threatening to collapse under the weight of decades of corrosion, the old whaling station is a testament to the fact that so much pollution does not just lie on the surface – it's dangerous right to the core.

The weather deteriorated as we waited our turn to go ashore. Clouds appeared and did battle with the sun, obscuring it more often than they allowed it to shine down on us as it had all morning. But this was it. This was Grytviken. This was Shackleton and his crew's last touch of humanity before they sailed into the vicious Southern Ocean, expecting hardships but completely unsuspecting of just what they would endure before they met with other men again. 'By endurance we conquer': Shackleton's family motto, which lent his ship her name. By *Endurance* we conquer. He did, and after her loss he conquered by

---

[14] The station was operated by Norway between 1904 and 1962, then by the Japanese between 1963 and 1965. Operations ceased in 1966.

continuing. To conquer the ice is Herculean. To conquer it when it has destroyed that little shell which protects you from it is something beyond.

I think I should have liked to have met Endurance. Despite the raging wind *Nordnorge* seemed very still, as though cocooned in her own reverence.

I think I should have liked to have met her master.

He's still here, at Grytviken, buried in the whalers' cemetery just outside the village. This was where Shackleton died in 1921, reaching for the south yet again. No matter what Antarctica did to him he just kept going back, an abused lover perpetually returning to the arms of a mistress not only possessed of a heart of ice but whose entire *being* was ice.

Thomas MacLeod was there too.

The expedition continued under the command of Frank Wild who has also been second in command during the Endurance expedition. The Boss would have wanted that, and no-one knew that better than Wild.

His grave faces south.

'I believe a man should strive to the utmost for his life's prize.'

The epitaph can only be seen from outside the cemetery.

(It hadn't been mentioned in any briefings on board the ship, but Dad knew it was there. He tried to tell some of the others about it but they didn't seem to care.)

I crouched by the headstone, reading tributes left there.

I had nothing to leave. I had a tiny volume of *Hamlet* bound in green leather in my pocket, but why would he want that? He certainly appreciated Shakespeare, but Robert Browning was his favourite, as intimated by the words on the back of his headstone.

We're almost there.

What do you mean, Boss?

I thought I *was* there.

Just a little further. You cannot find the living among the dead.

He was there, a few feet below that marked out rectangle. The last mortal remains of a man who on so many occasions had just refused to die. The hero, the leader; the husband, the father; the explorer, the seaman, the frustrated poet. And in that windy cemetery at the world's end, standing up and taking a step back, all I could find to say was 'He kicked the ice's butt.'

When I lamented my ineloquence to my dad he assured me, 'That was just fine.'

It was only a few days later that I realised, as the credits of that evening's movie rolled, that I had forgotten something...

We left the cemetery by a path that took us around the back of the buildings that had once been the dwelling places of up to 1300 people, away from the prowling JCBs. 'Stick to the path' had been hammered home forcefully during our pre-landing briefing yesterday and guides were positioned at various points to act as marshals. As we prepared to hop across a ditch a young seal came flopping towards us curiously. He showed no real intention of stopping, just paused to take stock of these new-comers now that he could see them better. The guide stationed there was Arnau, the Spanish chap who gave lectures on the history of Antarctic exploration and had to suffer surround-sound correction of his English from the middle-aged American women. He was busy deploying anti-seal defensive weaponry – a long stick which he waved in front of the animal's nose with occasional stabs at the ground just in front of it.

'What do we do if he comes any closer?' Dad asked.

Without taking his attention from the seal or the stick Arnau replied in all seriousness, 'Get ready to run.'

But the pup didn't come any closer. Perhaps he thought that these lumbering red creatures were trying to escape the aggressive yellow one, and he was doing something helpful by distracting it while the terrorised herd scrambled clumsily across the ditch to safety. Or maybe he just thought we were all completely insane and so would not make suitable playmates. He got bored and flopped away, leaving Arnau standing there with his stick.

Before us now was a patch of ground that had most certainly once been a cultivated rectangle. I grinned. The purpose it had served before the time of abandonment was still obvious. Dad had got his 'Most Southerly Steam Engine in the World.' This, for me, was a version of the same trophy: the Most Southerly Football Pitch in the World, its goal posts still standing, and indeed looking to be in better condition than many a pitch I'd played on.

Ossie Ardiles' time as a player for Tottenham Hotspur pre-dates mine as a fan by a couple of years. I first became aware of him as the somewhat ineffective manager who was sacked in 1994 after just one season in charge.

A sad departure for a man who, as a player, had done so must for the club. Sad also that after the 1982 World Cup, where he had played for his native Argentina, he had felt unable to return to England and had spent a year in 'exile' in Paris , playing for Paris Saint Germain, before coming back to White Hart Lane. Such hostility surrounds England-Argentina matches, most of that fury now emanating from people who either were not born at the time of the Conflict, or, like me, were toddling around their back gardens stumbling over plastic 'Spain 82' footballs. But when those same Argentineans play their domestic football for an English club, they may achieve cult status and attract hero-worship. So why do they become villains when they don the pale blue and white stripes if their English teammates are wearing red or white?

In 2008 Ossie Ardiles was inducted into the Tottenham Hotspur Hall of Fame. And rightly so. But I never said he was a hero.

Beyond the football pitch, a little Lutheran church snuggled at the base of a mountain which dwarfed it vertiginously. It was all decked out in white, striking quite a contrast against the ubiquitous crumbling oil tanks. In this little church, thirteen civilians, staff from the scientific station, had taken refuge during the Battle of King Edward Point before being rounded up onto helicopters by the victorious Argentine forces, who carried them off as prisoners of war. They were released unharmed when the conflict came to an end.

One pastor lamented that the local population had little interest in what he had to offer. But the mere presence of the church gives away much about the whaling station. Look at any Ordinance Survey map and find any settlement of size from the tiniest village still soldiering on since medieval times to sprawling cosmopolitan conurbations, and you'll see they all have a church. Grytviken was more than a factory – it was a community. A community united by its isolation, made up of people with the same dangerous and thankless job – after all who thought of the whaler when they lit their lamp as darkness fell? – a job which would be considered by posterity to be cruel and inhumane? 'Save the Whale,' the placards read, but it seems to be acceptable to consider humans the scum of the earth.

After a Post Office at Port Lockroy and a (closed) tourist information centre at Arctowski Base, a museum at Grytviken doesn't seem in any way out of the ordinary. And I knew it was there. I had read a book by one of its curators, Pauline Carr, a couple of months earlier. She and her husband had sailed around the world in their yacht, *Curlew*, a 28-footer who would be a hundred years old this year, for twenty-five years before deciding to make South Georgia their home. I had hoped that I would get to see *Curlew*, but Pauline told me that she is now at the National Maritime Museum in Cornwall.

A temporary staff member under the Carrs' employ was busy cleaning and restoring finds. Imagine *that* for a gap year placement. I'm one of those annoying people who actually read things in museums, but I had learned at Port Lockroy that this was not a luxury one has when a shipload of tourists descends. Although the continuous-stream landing method had people trickling from the cemetery, avoiding the seals and passing the football pitch towards the church, the museum had become a bottleneck. Nobody seemed to want to go through it. I found myself squeezed into one corner after another and eventually, after almost falling over a replica Scott-era sledge I was squeezed out of the door. An early example of a harpoon gun was standing there patiently awaiting the attention of the curators' assistant, so I fell over that instead.

In the harbour *Nordnorge* lay at anchor bathed in sunlight and framed by the superstructures of *Petrel* and *Albatross*. The two whaling ships seemed to gaze at me mournfully, imploring me to tell them where their masters were, what had happened to them and when they would be back.

They're not coming back.

They were so small.

For many of us today our window on whaling is tinted by environmental activist propaganda. Regardless of whether they are 'right' or not, it is still propaganda. We are presented with images of enormous vessels, usually Japanese, that look like close cousins of aircraft carriers, their decks awash with blood. But any whale worth its blubber could have capsized either, or both, of these little ones as soon as look at them. And modern Norwegian whaling ships aren't much bigger. In the era to which these two tiny vessels belonged, whaling *was* an unequal contest – in favour of the whale.

We picked up some passengers at Grytviken. They were thumbing a lift to the Falklands. Their ride was supposed to have been a fisheries protection vessel, but they'd made an arrest and so couldn't detour to South Georgia to come and collect them. The fine for poaching in the sub-Antarctic waters is £1.8 million. £1.8 million or they sink the ship. This is a frontier. These seas are so remote that the regular codes of conduct don't apply, can't apply. These may be harsh waters with a harsh history, but justice abides. Justice as swift and dispassionate as the ocean over which it presides.

This little patch of ground doesn't look like it was a war zone twenty-two years ago. Bullet holes still visible have blended with the decay of the intervening years. But Time ceased here when the whalers left, the abandoned legacy of that by-gone era oblivious to the shell-fire and mines and people shooting at each other. Grytviken doesn't care. Its native dilapidation has absorbed all obvious traces of war. To think that people should have fought over this relic of an industry which we now frown upon, not only steeped in blood and death but in human loneliness – *no damn good anywhere else* – with no noble or redeeming quality but that the sovereign power refused to abandon it… and that gives this savage lump of rock more dignity than the most fertile of lowlands or richest of goldmines. South Georgia may have in it no profit but the name, but that name is made illustrious by its sovereign's care.

Fallen humanity, wretched and lost but for its Sovereign's love, such love that He sent His own Son to die on a cross…

Rust and asbestos, pollution and filth on the edge of the pristine White Continent. Depravity beyond the garden wall.

The whaling station at Grytviken, overrun by enemy forces, has been redeemed, but remains just outside of Eden.

CHAPTER 12
Stromness

I t wasn't much to look at, really. Even among lesser landscapes it would not have been particularly impressive. Only the knowledge of what had happened here nearly ninety years ago gave this place identity.

This was Journey's End on the Shackleton Trail. Stromness – a tiny whaling community at the tail-end of the earth about as isolated and godforsaken as we in our 21st century of airliners and video conferencing can imagine. Yet what a cradle of civilisation it must have been for those who were undoubtedly the most isolated men on the planet.

By the time we'd landed the pale blue sky to which I had awoken (and chided myself for not waking sooner) was beginning to cloud over, a dull grey indifference, as though the island were in a sulk.

How magnificent am I now?

But I was used to sulky islands. I had lived on one for eighteen years.

I thought of the other Stromness, at the other end of the world, and wondered if those men who came here to scrape a livelihood among these fierce southern seas saw as I had the reflection of their own island here and so named their community for its largest town. Or perhaps they were simply homesick. This is not *New* Stromness. Leith lies a little to the north. And to the south, just over a headland, is Husvik, also bearing the name of a town so far away and yet in its elements so close. Lewis was a territory of Norway until 1266 and the ties between the Scots and the Norse are written into the map of South Georgia.

Even in meteorological mediocrity this place *was* magnificent, not so much now for the immense, proud majesty of Nature, unsullied by human hands, but because it brought out the indomitable courage of the human heart. Here, Man, so utterly insignificant, had challenged Nature and Nature had yielded. Or here three men had survived all Nature's attempts to halt them, and so she had conceded to them.

Ahead of us was the last half mile or so of the epic journey we had been following for almost two weeks. Dad and I walked in silence along a seasonal riverbed, which in spring would carry meltwater from the glacier that smothers the South Georgia's interior. Mostly dry now in the southern autumn, it became a road reaching out to the mountains that hemmed that glacier in, holding back its cruel grip from the coast. Shackleton's Highway.

Looking towards those mountains, I imagined them – three exhausted travellers picking their way down the slope pointed out to us by our guide.

They had landed on the 'wrong' side of the island, separated from the whaling stations by South Georgia's mountainous and then uncharted backbone. It was as though upon seeing them achieve a feat of navigation so great that some malevolent Fate was determined to confound them just as salvation hove into view.

And that was when He joined them, the Fourth Man whose presence they each felt as they made their way across those mountains. Yet none of them spoke of it to the others until many years afterwards.

I couldn't help but wonder if perhaps Scott had not insisted that Darwin be read as a counter to Bowers' passages from the Bible a similar presence might not have joined him on the Great Ice Barrier four years previously.

This was as good a place as any. The path of the dry river wound in to the mountains behind us, the governor's house to our right. I carefully searched my camera bag and took out the bread roll and film canister (thoroughly washed the night before) of orange juice that I had smuggled away from breakfast.

I return to Scotland four times a year for Communion, to the church where three generations of my family have worshipped. This weekend was to have been one such pilgrimage. Inspired by Apollo astronaut Buzz Aldrin, who took Communion on the moon, I had decided that being a mere 6000 miles away (compared to a quarter of a million) was no excuse not to observe the rite.

Dad knew what I was planning to do; he had also partaken of a lonely Communion in the north of Norway once. He watched me break the bread roll in two and I passed him one of the pieces.

Christ said *This is my body broken for you. Do this in remembrance of me.*

And that is what Communion is – remembrance.

We ate the bread in silence then I opened the little cylinder of juice. I took a sip and passed it to Dad. He sipped also.

Where two or three are gathered together in my name there will I be Christ had said. And just as Shackleton, Worsely and Crean were sure that four had crossed those mountains, I believed that there were three now standing less than half a mile from the foot of them.

Meeting that ragged trio in the doorway of that white building but a few hundred yards off, the governor of the Stromness whaling station could have been forgiven for mistaking them, like the gatekeeper of Dante's Mount Purgatory, for souls escaped from Hell, who had 'slipped the eternal prison-house.'[xli] And in Dante's theology, the core of Hell being ice, that was exactly what they were.

Perhaps it might be truer to say that with us there was also a fourth presence. Even as he was sent to me, I was seeking him, seeking someone who had come back alive, not once but three times. And even then, it was not his enemy-lover/lover-enemy who had dealt the final blow.

One who had refused to die, but succumbed in the end now pointed me towards the One who willingly offered up His life…and refused to stay dead.

Said Virgil to the gatekeeper,

'…Heaven's design

ORION IS UPSIDE DOWN

Brought me; a lady stooped from bliss to pray
My aid and escort for this charge of mine.'[xlii]

We proclaim the death of Christ until He comes or calls us to Himself.

I do not know how long it will be before I stand on the shores of the Glassy Sea. But I do know that in that interim of eternity which we call Life I will never be alone.

Communion. Wherever we may find ourselves, wherever I may find myself, faith makes one of the many.

It could hardly have been more perfect, standing in the trickle that still fought its way to the sea along the dry bed of a seasonally mighty river, a stone's throw from the white governor's house - white, a suitable hue for the salvation that that building represented for Shackleton and his companions all those years ago.

He did it. He came to fetch me, in that dark wood. I followed him to the ice at the centre of hell, my hell - ah but there I did find such good - and out the other side, the slow ascent of Mount Purgatory, the Antipodes - land created when the earth fled from falling Satan, to the earthly paradise, to Eden, or what remains in this corrupted world, a sinless continent, untainted by fallen Man. He had called me through time and space from half a world and almost a century away and at last he had met with me, in a windswept cemetery surrounded by the bones of many brave men.

And now I know that there is no ice to be found upon that Glassy Sea where she now is.

'The old, old love in all its mastering might...
...That high power which pierced me, heart and reins,
Long since, when I was but a child in years.'[xliii]

He has served the Lady. And now it is time to hand me over.

..e'en as a pilgrim, bent on his return...[xliv]

The mad Captain Kirkwood rants to a terrified ship's boy about 'the great navigators' who 'sought out the hidden corners of the world,' telling him,

'They did not think the passage out important, but the journey home. That was when they drew their contours and learnt their souls' identity. The maps they drew were of themselves...'[xlv]

Songe d'Automne circles and dances in the currents of the wind.
It's time to go home.

I don't know where that is.
Home is not necessarily where the heart is. It is often where the hurt is.

It was probably the first time a 35mm film canister had been used for a communion cup.

Now orphaned of my Virgil, I trudged the path back towards what passed for civilisation on this scrap of island coast, the buildings that made up Stromness itself, more aware than ever that we were walking in the footsteps of heroes. The word 'hero' has been devalued of late. Recently it has come to be almost synonymous with mere 'survivor' or to be applied to those whose achievements may be admirable and impressive but are by no means heroic. Just as South Georgia has reclaimed the concept of magnificence from a jaded humanity, it has defined anew heroism as it ought to be understood.

We arrived back at the ruins of the whaling station to find that the seals had all decided to go to the beach and were forming an obstacle course between the Red Penguins and the Polar Cirkle boats. The indigenous penguins presented a further trip hazard, but this was one that moved. It seemed a little ironic that although we were falling over animal life, sometimes literally, which Must Not Be Interfered With, though they had no qualms about interfering with us, we were not allowed to approach the remains of human influence. Like Grytviken, Stromness is infested with asbestos. Fortunately, unlike its penguin population, the ruins at Stromness are not self-ambulatory.

The wind was picking up, tearing little white tufts from the crests of the waves over which we sped as we made our way back to the ship. Her orientation was quite different from when we had left, turned to offer some shelter for the returning Polar Cirkle boats, but even from the shore I had noticed that she was pivoting around her anchor, twisting and straining at her chain, like a dog with some wolf-blood – tame and faithful, but suddenly answering some instinctive desire for freedom. Not surprising. The surrounding shoreline was littered with wrecks and the weather was becoming threatening, even in this relatively sheltered bay. She was scared, and like any frightened animal just wanted to flee, to be out in the open sea away from those malevolent cliffs.

People were still on the beach, lying down among the carpet of wall-to-wall seals. When a boat arrived, a small group would get up and stagger towards it, bent almost double by the wind. How quickly the weather had changed! I thought of Shackleton and his men, setting off on what had been a fine, clear night. This had been a fine, clear morning. If winds like those whipping the beach had struck the mountains that night they would have been blown right off.

Boatload by boatload, the windswept ship's complement returned, but for the first time *Nordnorge* seemed indifferent, paying no heed to her little boats and their valiant struggle not to tip their cargoes into the restless sea. She was too caught up in her own struggle against the worsening elements and, as it turned out, one of her own appendages.

Tomas's long and slightly garbled tannoy announcement made about an hour after the last wind-battered passengers were back on board roughly translated as: 'The anchor is stuck.'

'Slightly captive' was a euphemism a colleague of mine had once used for machinery in a similar position.

A crowd soon gathered on Deck 5 looking down into the forecastle, watching a crewman in a blue boiler suit move amongst the machinery, inspecting it and occasionally peering over the side into the water beneath. *Nordnorge* was slowly orbiting the point where her port anchor was trapped by the legacy left by the Stromness whalers on the seabed. Her chain had been let out in some attempt to disentangle it, but her slow dance only twisted it further. The easy-does-it approach was abandoned.

Winches rattled into life to take up the slack then twelve thousand horses bound up in steel skin strained at the chain.

Frigjør meg! Frigjør meg! Let me go!

The rise and fall of the ship on the swell when the engines stopped could have been taken for heavy breathing. *Nordnorge* tried once more to free herself by means of her own raw power. Then she lay still, and settled meekly on the deep swell, her strength bested, captive in this treacherous bay, and silently begged her crew for help.

The crewman in the forecastle had been joined by a shipmate in a red boiler suit and they huddled over the chain-stop, which stuttered furiously as a fresh attempt was made to let the chain out. It crunched to a halt with the screech of tortured metal.

I peered down, my fascination with The Machine driving my curiosity even as my affinity with it made me want to pull away from the sight of a ship in any sort of distress, however trivial.

The twisted chain was trapped somewhere inside the mechanism. And that mechanism was not moving.

Then the sledgehammer appeared.

Looked like one Thor might have traded in for a less cumbersome model.

The crewman in red hoisted it and brought it crashing down on the misbehaving machinery. Then he did it again. The winches screamed, like banshees welded to the deck, but the chain remained jammed in the stop. More hammering. A crowbar made an entrance, then an exit. Another crewman appeared. The winches were provoked to scream again to demonstrate the non-cooperation. Red Boiler Suit once more took up the hammer and pounded the unfortunate chain-stop. Hydraulic fluid spurted over the forecastle. *Nordnorge* was bleeding.

If the chain-stop hadn't been broken before, it certainly was now.

An officer arrived and shooed us all back inside, sparing the ship and her crew the indignity of an audience while the solution was implemented.

The chain was severed inches above the water line.

After three hours trying to free herself, *Nordnorge* sailed despondently away, leaving among the detritus of the whaling era of the early twentieth century that littered the seabed in Stromness Bay a large black anchor, circa 1997.

The chain on which I keep my piece of *Titanic*'s coal around my neck broke.

I had been getting out of my outdoor gear after being shooed away from the deck overlooking the forecastle along with everyone else when I found the chain caught in my scarf. I removed it very carefully from around my neck. The coal is in a tiny cage and if it fell on the floor I knew it would spring open and the coal would fall out. Finding it would not have been easy. I took the chain and cage from my scarf, then wrapped them up in tissue paper and put the little bundle in the film canister that had just served as a communion cup. If it had not got caught on my scarf, would it have been caught on some other item of clothing before falling? Would it perhaps have gone down inside my sweater? Or would it have just fallen out from underneath my jacket? And would it have been such a bad thing, to leave it on South Georgia?

As I had bowed my head before that headstone, his shade still beside me, would I have felt or done anything differently had I known that the following day his presence would leave me and return to it, this time to await the Last Trumpet and the resurrection of the body, when not only the earth but the sea shall give up her dead.

Now back in my comfortable but utilitarian cabin there was the void of a pilgrimage completed, the quieting of the restless soul that has completed its journey. The sacred ground has been stood upon, but the guide has departed.

Dante, weep not for Virgil's going...[reference]

She had sung to me again.

Why do I so enamour thee that thou turnest not to the fair garden which flowers beneath the rays of Christ?[xlvi]

Had God perhaps wanted her for Himself? Or was it necessary? Was judgement required upon the unnamed steward who uttered the blasphemy 'God Himself could not sink this ship'? I am glad his name is lost to history and I will never know, for if I did, I would blame him, and I cannot put my hand on my heart and say I could forgive.

Not in my eyes alone is Paradise.[xlvii]

What is it to be made 'in the image of God'? Two arms, two legs, one head? The writers of Star Trek: the Motion Picture got it right when they penned the line 'We create God in our own image.' God is first and foremost a Creator God. Surely it is creativity which makes us 'made in His image.' After all, we've seen other primates using tools, and technology is often considered to be the pinnacle of what makes us more than apes, but we've never seen one painting a landscape or carving a figurine for no reason other than it looks beautiful. The human creativity by which naval architects and marine engineers build things as beautiful as ships, as beautiful as *her*, is a gift from God, that particular gift which marks us as a special creation, separate from the animal kingdom. And didn't the blueprint for the first ever ship come directly from God?[15] The only other biblically recorded instances of such precise building instructions being given from on high are for the Tabernacle and the Temple, that were to be God's own dwelling places on earth.

I tried to stop thinking about it. It had been a warning shot across my bows. Perhaps I was guilty of venerating the relic. It had come so close, but He hadn't actually allowed me to lose it.

The delay meant that the afternoon's landing in Fortuna Bay had to be abandoned and the penguin enthusiasts had to make do instead with observing the creatures from the deck. Given the size of some of the camera lenses the ornithologists waved around, I don't think distance would really be too much of an impediment to their photographs.

Dad hadn't managed during either landing so far to take the threatened photograph of me next to a king penguin ('...for the purpose of height comparison!'). I suspected that that may have been on his agenda for Fortuna Bay. However, one budding artist saw the funny side and displayed on the notice board their interpretation of the penguins' disappointment at receiving no visitors that afternoon.

It was now almost 800 nautical miles to the Falkland Islands. That evening's movie was in German and about whales, and I didn't fancy it much so after dinner, I made my way to the bow, the scene of the afternoon's excitement. Deserted now, nothing to see here. *Nordnorge* and I kept each other company.

The crew had cleaned up her bloody nose, and the only evidence that remained of the sudden violence was patches of exposed steel on the chain-stop. It looked like nothing a lick of paint wouldn't fix, but I couldn't help wondering what sort of mess of mangled metal might lie within. Maybe I imagined it, but I was sure the ship was listing to starboard, a sort of nautical limp.

Nordnorge seemed profoundly embarrassed, but her sister would soon steal the thunder that Thor's Hammer had bestowed upon her. Imagine the conversation when *Nordnorge* came to *Nordkapp*'s rescue at Deception Island:

...they won't let you come back
They let you come back.
I only lost an anchor.
At least my crew didn't make things worse.

---

[15] Genesis 6:14-16, when God told Noah to build the Ark

115

Samuel Taylor Coleridge, whose Ancient Mariner had been lately on my mind, developed the concept of 'suspension of disbelief.' That is, that a person can ignore the logical impossibility of fantastic elements of literature. More recently this has been expanded, encapsulating the ability to over-look the limitations of stage and screen. Thus we overcome the difficulty of a world of black-and-white, many days, months or years passing in minutes or the rational impossibility of spacecraft landing on the White House lawn or finding a country in the back of a wardrobe.

And it is a concept also demonstrated in our ability to see a multitude of different roles played by the same actor and yet each time believe him to be the man he is currently playing. But when that man is someone with whose character and attributes you are so familiar, whose face you know so well, and he suddenly inhabits another body and face and voice that you know well, it is not enough to simply lay aside disbelief. You find yourself employing Orwellian thought processes, *double-think*, 'to hold simultaneously two ideas which cancel out knowing them to be contradictory yet believing in both of them.'

But it could not have been otherwise. Word on the street had it that when the man chosen for the lead role met the producer he was told there was no script yet, because if he turned it down, there would be no movie.

One slightly cynical definition of 'genius' is to hold in one's mind simultaneously two contradictory ideas. The mark then of a truly great actor then is to make geniuses of his audience.

The evening's movie was Channel 4's *Shackleton*, with the enormously talented – and devastatingly attractive – Kenneth Branagh in the lead. There was some confusion caused by the syzygy of the alternation between English and German films each evening and the opening scene (in which Shackleton is delivering a lecture in German) and a few left the 'cinema.' Their loss.

The movie is superb. Much of the script has been taken from direct speech quoted in the books that some of the expedition members wrote upon their return, and several shots begin with recreations of Frank Hurley's photographs – particularly evocative is the football match they played on the ice, with Shackleton in goal. (I used to play football with my boss on Tuesday lunchtimes. Fortunately we played for the same team.)

Mr Branagh is, of course, utterly perfect and characteristically flawless in the role, so much so that I was on occasion quite disturbed to see, for all intents and purposes, my hero looking like someone else who I had on a pedestal. Then, just to really confuse me, *The Merchant of Venice* found its way in:

> *First go with me to church and call me wife...*
> *...You shall have gold to pay the petty debt twenty times.*

116

My purse, my person, my extremest means lie all unlock'd to your occasion…

For some reason this scene was missing from the American release, which was screening here. It was somehow conspicuous in its absence.

But what happens when that ability to willingly put aside one's rational disbelief fails, not outwardly such that one can no longer believe the fiction, but inwardly, an implosion that results in the inability *not* to believe the fiction? Little holes open in the universe and suddenly the 'It's only a movie' mantra doesn't work anymore. The reflection of life in art is no stranger. But the final straw comes in knowing that the fiction is not fiction at all.

Frighted by no false fire, I.

I had hitherto been unable to sit through *Shackleton*, not in its entirety. The crushing of *Endurance* by the pack ice is depicted so graphically that I had bolted from the room every time, and no amount of telling myself it was a set and not a ship made any difference.

But I had made a conscious decision.

This time I was going to stay.

My choice.

I will not look away.

If I look away, it's won.

I will show no fear.

I didn't have my coal. That too was conspicuous in its absence.

This wasn't the first time something like this had happened. That's why I'd always run. Because I knew what was coming.

One application of the suspension of disbelief is the ability to believe in black-and-white movies. So when something you've only ever seen in monochrome explodes from the screen in a blaze of glorious Technicolor…

The model was perfect. Every bench, every bollard, every capstan. Every railing, every window frame, every porthole on the port side… I had only ever seen her in black-and-white before. This was what she had really looked like.

People asked me, did I cry during *Titanic*?

Yes, I did. But not when other people did. When the ship was leaving Southampton, and a crane shot comes over her forecastle, travelling aft along the boat deck, I knew it all. And later, when I realised that I could not tell the difference between the model and actual wreck footage. I couldn't tell what was her and what was a lump of plastic. Amongst all his historical felonies committed in the making of that film, I've never forgiven James Cameron for that.

Dost thou come to whine? To outface me with leaping in her grave?

Too much of water hast thou, and so I forbid my tears.

The wrong Ophelia.
   Get on your knees and pray for *Shackleton*.
   On the forecastle, the anchor waits.
   The credits roll.
   ….I have forgotten to say thank you.

Interlude

The next morning the albatrosses came.
   Great formless forms of white that weaved side to side across the wake of the ship in sine waves of divine grace.
   The whiteness unfurled into wings as those birds of good omen swept closer and closer to the stern. *Nordnorge* once again carried a cargo of souls but no longer was the infernal ferrymen at her helm. Ushering us northwards, that deepest Cold behind, it seemed indeed that the Angel of the Lord was our pilot. And like Dante's Angel of the Lord, they 'scorned the instruments of earth,'[xlviii] on the wing for years without touching ground - or water - 'twixt shores that span so vast an ocean's girth.'[xlix] Did the adventurers of the Heroic Age feel as they left that frozen waste of water and land and ice that an angel now guided them home in the form of another living creature come to greet them from lands they would soon approach?
   These angelic heralds soared between sea and sky, urging the ship of souls onwards through the void between hell and heaven, their winged dance so sublime that surely no mortal being could achieve it made possible by the naturally high lift coefficient of their high aspect-ratio wings.
   For a moment I focused on the rhythmic vibration in the deck-plates beneath my feet, the forces of the cyclic action of the engines propagating up through the structure – the ship's heartbeat. And there was the world from my strange inverted angle. I saw the mechanical in the organic and felt the organic in the mechanical.
   But in these majestic birds, nature had done without numbers what Man had taken centuries of analysis to uncover. For four years it had been deemed a vital part of my university education that I be able to prove mathematically what in these magnificent creatures just *was*. The result of millions of years' worth of random mutations. Or is God a mathematician?
   Mathematics and science and physics do not deny the existence of God. They support it.
   Nature is mechanical. God is an aeronautical engineer.
   We talk about 'playing God' when scientists interfere with life in its earliest stages. But the God who makes hearts beat and eyes see is the same God who gave the albatross its mathematically perfect wings.

Orville and Wilbur 'played God' as much as any potential Victor Frankensteins of the future.

We have no wings but found a way to fly.

The same set of equations govern the wings of the albatross and the Airbus, the minds of God and Man touching. We are, after all, made in His image.

'How likely do you think that is? He had a dream and went to find them?'

Loud Englishman had found a friend, and their common ground appeared to be volume. They weren't that far away, only two tables over, but I don't think they'd been able to overhear *our* conversation. I'd managed to ignore them thus far, but Dad had gone to get another glass of water and I no longer had any distraction. Unfortunately you can't shut your ears the way you can your eyes. And ears are omnidirectional.

Loud Englishman was agreeing with his friend's scepticism over the scene in Channel 4's *Shackleton* where Frank Worsley explains his reasons for wanting to join the Expedition.

I fought the urge to go over and point out to them that the script was superbly accurate and that Worsley *did* claim his motivation to have been inspired by what he called an 'absurd dream.' Their ignorance was doing nobody any harm, and it was not my job to enlighten them.

How does God send His angels? Before joining Shackleton's expedition, Frank Worsely, master of *Endurance* and navigator extraordinaire, had a dream that he was sailing along Burlington Street and it was full of ice. He was so affected by this dream that he felt compelled to go and see if there was anything out of the ordinary there. He found the offices of the Imperial Trans-Antarctic Expedition and knew he had to sign up. Ancient texts are full of 'And the Lord spoke to So-And-So in a dream.' Did God send Worsely to Shackleton so that he could lead those men to safety? Out here in this wilderness of water I believe I came to understand something of how the omniscience of God and human free will co-exist. God knew that Shackleton would fail; yet, in the word of Winston Churchill's telegraph, He allowed him to 'proceed.' But although He knew what would happen, He made sure that they would be taken care of. God lets us make mistakes, but won't let us come to true harm if it's not yet our time. Unlike Scott, who insisted that Darwin be read aloud in the tent as a counter-weight to Henry Bowers' Bible readings, Shackleton had a Christian faith. But even agnostic Scott, after witnessing the peace and dignity with which Bowers met the inevitable, wrote in his final letter to his wife, 'Try to make [our son] believe in God – it is comforting.' I like to believe that Scott might have come to some sort of faith in the end. Antarctica *is* God's continent, the last portion of creation as He intended it, and I don't blame Him for wanting to keep it for Himself.

CHAPTER 13
Stanley

You know how when you dream, sometimes you're in a place, like your old school, but it doesn't look anything like your old school, but you know that's where you are? Well, I had just woken up to find myself on a ship tied to Number 1 Pier in Stornoway Harbour fifteen years ago.

The pier at Port Stanley didn't look like that old pier at Stornoway, but it *felt* like it.

We disembarked by the gangway (this now appearing the height of civilisation) into a place that although I had never been there before was absurdly familiar. The white island sky, the open gangway, the pier, the ships, and the smell of where the sea meets the land. Buses were sitting on the pier waiting to take us to Stanley itself. The dream-like incongruity continued as we boarded the bus and were addressed in an accent unmistakably English (yet difficult to place *where* in England) when I had been momentarily expecting some form of Leodhaiseach lilt. The sense of humour was also unmistakably English. During his introductory remarks when our tour guide came to languages he announced that he spoke English and that he spoke English loudly. Oh dear, another one. I hoped they wouldn't find themselves engaged in conversation which might turn into a battle of decibels. Such contests are entertaining between ships (especially when the ships are operated by the same shipping line) but between humans become rather irritating very quickly.

The bus tour took us out to Sparrow Cove. I don't remember anything of what the guide told us about it as the bus rumbled along (it was certainly a lot healthier than the one that had conveyed us around the environs of Ushuaia) but whatever he said it certainly did not prepare me.

'Ships' graveyard' may sound a slightly clichéd term, but I can think of no other.

The cove was littered with decaying hulks. There must have been dozens. A wreck lying where she has sunk is one thing, but these poor wretches had just been scuttled and abandoned here. They had not even been given the dignity of a final voyage to the breakers' yard, but left here in this hideous mass grave. Nameless now, I wondered if those who had known them in their working lives would still be able to identify them. I hoped that they wouldn't, because it would surely break their hearts. But they had once had names, funnels, masts, superstructures and crews, people who had loved and sailed and maintained them. And enough people had loved one former denizen of that maritime limbo to free her and bring her home alive.

It was strange. The bottom of the dry dock was warm, and shirt-sleeves comfortable. I looked up through the panels of shimmering optical illusion through which the sun of the late August bank holiday was bidding a valedictorian salute to the summer, as though I was looking up from the bottom of the sea. Yet on this seabed I was breathing and walking and whispering.

Oh you poor thing. You poor, beautiful thing. Does it hurt?

No, *the ship replied.* Not anymore. It has healed well.

The same magnificent trick of water and light that made this look like the seabed made it appear from the surface as though the SS Great Britain *was afloat in her dock, just waiting for the tide to take her out into the Avon, the Bristol Channel and the Atlantic Ocean once again. And her engine turning over, waiting, brand new reconstruction, exact in all except materials, built by Rolls Royce using modern lightweight materials used in aerospace. But that would never happen. Her iron hull was riddled with holes, just little ones mostly, from natural corrosion, like you see on abandoned cars. But on her starboard side, running right down her flank was a great strip of metal, crudely riveted and welded in place. A field dressing, applied before the gargantuan operation to bring her home from Sparrow Cove. But it was the wound that it covered that was tearing at my own heart. The intention had been to scuttle her by breaking her in two. It hadn't been successful, thankfully, but when the explosives had detonated a section of her hull running from her bulwarks down to her waterline was split.*

Ships split in two get to me almost as much as ships trapped in ice.

I didn't ask her if it did hurt. I didn't want to know the answer.

She was awesome. There was almost nothing that ship hadn't done, almost nowhere she hadn't been. She had had a phenomenally long working life of ninety years. She was incredible. And she had been left to rot among other discarded hulks on an island in the backend of Beyond. But even there, in that suspension of semi-death, she, a merchant ship all her life, served her country, her country's fleet, in its time of need. SS Great Britain *was an unexpected and unsung hero of the first major naval battle of the Second World War.*

During the Battle of the River Plate, HMS Exeter, *one of three Royal Navy Cruisers hunting the German battleship* Admiral Graf Spee, *was seriously damaged. Plates were taken from* Great Britain's *hull and used to dress* her *wounds. A transplant. Giving of herself, her own steel - her own flesh - so that another could keep fighting for the country whose name she bore.*

I took a last look around Sparrow Cove, swallowing my sorrow, before getting back onto the bus. Five days ago I had never seen a wreck. Now I felt as though I'd seen a lifetime's worth. These fallen sparrows. 'Are not two sparrows sold for a penny? And yet not one of them falls to the ground but your Heavenly Father knows about it.'[1] What special providence is there in their fall? Are they there too, perhaps, afloat once again on the Glassy Sea.

It eased the grief a little to know that one had been salvaged - recalled to life - and this was the result of no grand political gesture paying empty homage to the great engineering heritage that is ours. It was the love of human beings which brought her home.

But a little part of her remains. One of her masts lies on display by the esplanade at Stanley. She has gone home, but she has left a little piece of herself here, here where she suffered such indignity and was left to die.

'There's a satellite dish.'

Dad pointed it out.

For all its size, it would have been easy to miss, for it camouflaged itself against the whites and subtle greys of the sky.

'GST might be using that,' I replied.

One of the myriad diverse tasks I had performed on the project to which I was currently assigned had been to assess the coverage offered by various satellite groundstations once our bad-ass navigation satellite (whose name had contracted from Galileo Systems Test Bed Version 2 to the more manageable 'GST') was out of range of our own.

'Could you end up here as part of your work then?' Dad asked.

It wasn't likely – most of my work is with the space segment – but not impossible. I told him as much.

It's the question I've come to dread, mainly because I'm sure people think I'm fibbing when I answer.

'So, what do you do?'

I build satellites.

Someone has to.

'Oh. Do you design them?'

No. I build satellites. Make up the electrical connections. Check to see that they work properly.

I'm a glorified electrician, really.

I looked at the dish, finding myself in another of these moments of clarity. A couple of months ago, the Falklands groundstation had been just a facility on Satellite Tool Kit, the software we use to chart and simulate satellite orbits, and now here I was, staring at it.

It was the reverse of my experience at Ny Ålesund on Svalbard, appropriately enough, that being at the other end of the earth. We had seen the huge X-Band antenna dish from the ship, and I, still a naïve and optimistic student at the time, had photographed it eagerly, as I had anything connected with the industry I aspired to enter. A few short years later and I would be working every day with satellites which downlinked to it. From one extreme of the earth to the other, the world grew suddenly small.

GST didn't use the Falklands groundstation in the end.

Stanley isn't very big. It's home to four pubs, but after peeping round the door of the first we came across and discovering it to be full of people from the ship, we realised that they were all going to be like that. Lovely as they were, we had spent near enough the last fortnight with these people, and didn't particularly want to be elbowing them while we tried to sample Falklands pub fare. So we decided to go 'home' for lunch. It wasn't so bad being surrounded by people from the ship when we were actually on board the ship. They belonged *there*.

A crane had arrived on the scene when we got back to the pier. Unresisting as it was hauled from its resting place on *Nordnorge*'s forecastle, the spare anchor hung suspended from it, angular, black and severe against the white island sky, from which drops of heavy, determined rain were now falling. Injuries are not uncommon among ships of the Hurtigrute. They seem to suffer far more occupational hazards than most ships afloat. It's just then up to the crews and engineers to repair the damage, heal the wounds. When Bergen is at the other end of the world, you learn how necessary 'back to the yard' actually is. Port Stanley was a field hospital.

The crane deposited its burden on the pier next to where the chain, emerging from an opening in Nordnorge's bow and run out a considerable length, lay in a dejected-looking heap with a small knot of people gathered around it, among them Captain Hansen, keeping a close eye on what they were doing to his ship.

Although it felt like an invasion of privacy, I understood that it was actually quite a privilege to be able to witness this. Normally repairs to ships are carried out well away from curious on-lookers. Even in Norway, before the recent wave of health and safety measures that had accompanied Norway's decision to join the European Union (admittedly often not much more than the odd strategically-placed fence) swept the coast, passengers would never get this close to a repair in progress, except perhaps in the very far north. Only somewhere as truly isolated as the Falklands, thousands of miles from legislation, where the sea was still the sea and you just got on with it, was this possible.

I wondered how many of the other rubberneckers around me understood that. Cecilia did, of course. She carried around a heavy-duty digital SLR, her primary-school-teacher face rather incongruous peeping out from behind it.

I no longer regretted missing out on my pub lunch.

What the exact purpose of the pallet was I have no idea, but it must have been either ingenious or barmy. The crane was called back into play and lifted the anchor off the quay and put it down again on a wooden pallet that a forklift truck had delivered, hurriedly and precariously manoeuvred into place beneath it while it hung once again from the crane. Then the forklift drove its forks between the pallet's runners, the forks rose and met the resistance with a clunk. The pallet broke leaving the anchor sprawled once again on the quay, a mess of splintered wood crushed beneath it. The Norwegians looked bemused. The Falklanders didn't. The crane re-entred the mêlée as the lifting tool of choice.

123

But the anchor continued to defy all attempts at getting it into any sort of orientation that would allow the windlass within the bows of the ship to haul it in, and there was much humming and hawing and scratching of heads, although this time no-one produced a sledgehammer. They'd learned *that* lesson.

True to national stereotypes, Captain Hansen towered over the Port Stanley dockers, and his bowed head added an air of solemnity to their conference as they tried to decide What To Do Next.

With a resolute nod, by which his head disappeared below his shoulders, Captain Hansen straightened up and spoke into a walkie-talkie. A decision had been reached.

Everything happened very quickly.

The winches began to scream, but it was not the tortured screech that had rung out over Stromness three days ago. With the clatter of heavy metal on metal the slack in the chain rattled up inside the bow. The chain taught, there then hovered that precipitous moment as the anchor rose up and poised instantaneously between its weight being borne by the pier surface beneath it and the tension in the chain held by the ship's windlass, as though it was trying to resist the irresistible pull. But rise it did, a horizontal component of its velocity dragging it across the few feet of concrete to the pier's edge and then off, swinging violently towards the ship. The winches continued to howl, deeper now that they were pulling a massive tonnage of iron, and the anchor, suddenly exposed, vulnerable, no longer on the safe and solid pier, scrambled up the side of the ship like a frightened animal bolting for cover and disappeared inside *Nordnorge*'s bow. The whole process, from the moment the machinery started up until the anchor had vanished from view, had taken about twenty seconds.

Visiting the Falklands affected me profoundly.

The Conflict of 1982 is among my earliest memories.

Until then, it seemed, no-one really knew where the islands were. In my dad's words, 'Everybody thought they were somewhere near us.' And I could see why. If South Georgia had been Lewis mirrored in the equator, the Falklands were her image in that mirror, identical twins separated at birth to spend their lives at opposite ends of the planet, but with those subtle differences that in human beings would highlight the difference between nature and nurture.

Peat stacks. Almost everyone had one, and when I was young 'going to the peats' was an annual family event. On a Monday morning you could always tell when one of your friends had been 'at the peats' on Saturday (*never* on a Sunday) because they would be sunburned and covered in midgie bites. But there are peats and there are peats. The peats stacked up outside the houses on the outskirts of Stanley had been cut using the Norwegian method.

Norwegian peat stacks on the doppelgänger of a Scottish island. The Norse and the Celtic that had merged in the place-names on South Georgia were now coming together again in the rhythm of human life in the Falklands.

And there were the beaches. Another frustration of my trip to California had been that I was out-voted and instead of going to the mountains we spent a day sitting on a beach surrounded by hundreds of other people (and, by the way, it's all a lie – California is not teeming with beautiful people displaying a sight for all sore eyes scorched by the sun. Or if it is, none of them were on that beach). The Isle of Lewis has the most beautiful beaches in the world; such is its reputation, and such is the reality. When you go to the beach on Lewis if there are three other people on it it's crowded (even though they're often over a mile long) and you move on to the next one. And on the West Side, where they are most spectacular, the North Atlantic gallops up the sand, the first land it has encountered since Canada… the sight and the sound are truly awesome. Once you've seen the beaches of the Western Isles, you'll never sit content on you towel in your two square yards anywhere else again.

The Falklands have beautiful beaches too.

And all but one of them are minefields.

It broke my heart.

Something I took so completely for granted – the beach. What if those magnificent beaches, along which I have walked hundreds of miles, baptised time and time again by the ocean in which I swam and canoed and windsurfed, had been invisibly raped when I was three years old, and so that now at the age of twenty five my memories of a time when I would have been able to set foot on them would be as hazy as my memories now are of the Conflict itself.

During my weekly phone call home recently my Dad told me that they'd been to the beach the day before and of how my little nephew James had loved running around on the vast expanse of sand. As I write this, James is three. What if he were suddenly never to be able to do that again? Or, Heaven forbid, what if…?

The Argentineans had been driven from the islands, but their weapons remained. Weapons that are still primed and functioning. Twenty five years plus on, the invaders can still kill and injure people on these islands.

So had the islands really been liberated?

Had we really won?

It seems as though Falklands penguins are possessed of a similar indestructibility to that of Lewis sheep. After a close encounter which will usually wreck your car, a sheep on Lewis will get up and walk away, a little dazed but otherwise unharmed. The Falklands penguins are light enough that they can tread on as many landmines as they like without detonating them. Were this not the case, the beaches would probably all be safe by now, and the islands' penguin population listed as another casualty of war.

But what of the future? Recently there have been grumblings from Argentina once again, and this time the little patch of ground has far more profit in it than name, that profit being oil. But I can't help but wonder if our present prime minister would be as determined in the Islands' defence when there is something that the capitalist world considers worth fighting over as Thatcher was when there wasn't.

I thank God that Antarctica is protected by an international treaty. But what if massive mineral wealth were to be discovered beneath its ice-cap? How much respect would the parties of the treaty have for it then? McMurdo Base, the American presence in Antarctica, is strong, dominant, even if they have stood upon the shoulders of unacknowledged giants to do it. And we have seen what has been inflicted on other parts of the world already for the sake of oil, and rumbles around the sub-Antarctic islands. But Antarctica is God's Continent, free until three hundred-odd years ago of messy humans, a mere eye-blink in geological time, the scale in which time is measured in Antarctica. Our presence there is permitted, tolerated, but that does not mean that that will be the case forever. A treaty, the product of fragile human diplomacy, protects Antarctica, and should that treaty be broken, I pray that God will protect His Continent and that our presence will be tolerated no longer.

It drizzled all afternoon. But here there were no hills of the mainland for it to obscure. The nearest 'mainland' was Argentina.

We visited Stanley's museum. Stornoway has a museum. To my shame, I have never visited it except on obligatory school outings.

Model ships in cases, beautiful, and I suffered severe modellers' envy. My kitchen table spends a lot of time converted to a shipyard. My model of *Titanic* was given to me for my seventh birthday and was a collaborative effort between my dad and myself. The model is in worse condition than the wreck, and I am in the process of replacing it, although the kits available now are grossly inferior to those produced, a-hem, twenty-plus years ago.

The ships in cases were mostly the vessels that had brought the first brave colonists to these islands. Among them was what I took to be a Cunarder I'd never heard of, red-and-black funnel, name ending –ia, the trademark of the Cunard line before Queen Mary came along. The story about the Cunard chairman telling King George V that they intended to name the new liner after 'the most illustrious lady who has ever been' (meaning Queen Victoria) and the King replying 'My wife would be delighted,' and thus the ship was named 'Queen Mary' is sadly apocryphal. But *Queen Victoria* would finally enter the fleet in 2008.

I collared a curator to ask about the mystery ship and discovered her not to be a Cunarder at all. And then I saw the letters.

Displayed on the wall were dozens of letters, some of them with crayon drawings at the bottom. They were from children. The children of Stanley, Stanley under foreign occupation. Ages 4, 5, 6. Just a couple of years older than I had been. Expressing in the way only such innocents can the true human feelings, hopes and fears (considerably more fears than hopes) of that morsel of history.

England football fans, before the next international against Argentina, read those letters. And then you'll know why you're so angry. Why they deserve a drumming, on the football pitch, as they did on the hills of these islands so far from the shores of old Blighty.

There are perhaps those who would think that the Falklands' location in the southern hemisphere (aren't we often told as children that the people in Australia stand on their heads?) has given them an upside-down outlook on politics. I cannot think of anywhere in the UK where one would find a 'Thatcher Drive.'

Blended in with my memories of the Conflict are Arthur Scargill and the Miners' Strike that followed close on its heels. The Iron Lady 'good', who refused to abandon that little outpost of the country she governed to a foreign aggressor, then the Iron Lady 'bad', who turned with the same force upon her own people, smashing the power of the trade unions and leaving the mining industry in tatters.

One man's liberator is another's oppressor, though in the grand vista of history few who've lived all their days in the United Kingdom truly know the meaning of the word 'oppression.'

At the beginning of the 1980s, Argentina was still under the last throes of a military dictatorship, stretching right back in one form or another to the country's independence from Spain in 1810. What might have been in store for the Islanders if Thatcher hadn't intervened? True, economic collapse, outrage at human rights abuses and increasing corruption in the government were signalling the end but it was the defeat by the British in 1982 that was the last straw, and the military dictatorship collapsed, leading to the country's first free elections in 1983 and the election of Raul Alfonsin as Argentina's first democratically elected president. What if the invasion had been successful and restored Leopoldo Galtieri's credibility? Not only would the Islanders who had lived under a British democracy fall suddenly under a dictatorship, but that dictatorship, clinging to life and only just holding on, would be resuscitated and prolonged by their very capture.

Perhaps it was not only the Falkland Islands that were liberated in June 1982.

The Liberation Monument on Thatcher Drive bears the name of every regiment of the British Armed Forces which fought, and the name of every ship that sailed from England as well, troop-carriers and battleships.

Dad pointed to it.

'There.'

Queen Elizabeth 2. The queen who went to war; as so many of the great liners did in both World Wars, and I wondered what would have become of

Titanic had she survived to see the Great War. Would she have been a hero, like her sister *Olympic*, who became a troop carrier with the distinction of being the only merchant ship to sink an enemy vessel during that war and earned the nickname Old Reliable. Or would she have been a casualty, like her other sister *Britannic*, commandeered as a hospital ship and struck a mine in the Adriatic, brought down by a weapon that wasn't meant for her in a place she was never meant to be.

But when I did see film of the *QE2* as she made her way through the Southern Ocean I was more afraid for her entering the ice-fields than I was for her entering the war zone, even though I knew that neither had harmed her.

***

'It's quite like Stornoway.'

This time, I was furious.

It wasn't Loud Englishman. I don't know who he was, but he was sitting at the table behind me.

'Did you hear that?' I hissed.

'What?'

Dad, sitting opposite me, was quite a bit further away from the Voice than I was and he was keeping his volume to levels acceptable in polite society so I wasn't surprised Dad hadn't heard.

'Bloke on the table behind me. He said Stanley was like Stornoway.'

I turned my head over the shoulder, glaring in case I should catch the perpetrator's eye, but there were two men sitting next to each other on that side of their table and it could equally have been either of them.

'When was *he* in Stornoway?' I muttered. 'Not any time recently.'

The berth at Port Stanley may have evoked strong memories of Number 1 Pier, but that is what they were – memories. Childhood memories. Number 1 Pier had not been used by the passenger ferry for nearly a decade. And Stanley itself was nothing like Stornoway, certainly not for the last twenty-five years. This was name-dropping. This man had been to the oh-so-remote Outer Hebrides and was trying to impress his fellow diners with it. I wondered if it was the same person I had heard vocalising to the ether, 'This is worse than the Minch.' Bet he didn't think that in the dining saloon on a ship in the Antarctic he would end up at a table next to someone who had been born there.

How *dare* he treat my island as some sort of trophy?

But I said nothing more. Did not approach him. What would I have said anyway?

The anger which at the time could bend no words to its will, filtering through almost the full range of human emotion, distilled finally into eloquence... at 30,

000 ft. on the plane back to Madrid. Dad told me later that he had thought I was going to be sick as I rummaged through the pockets in front of both our seats looking for the only blank paper readily available - the little bags provided by the airline for that purpose.

'Pen! Pen!'

Realising that the sick-bag was to be put to a more noble use than that which nature intended, Dad fished a pen out of his pocket and handed it to me.

I began scribbling.

Every tide and ocean swell the journey we must make to find ourselves as the ocean rolls a multitude of weary souls…

Island rain
In peat bog veins
Through aeons that have been and are to come.
Beneath primeval ice
Adamantine Gneiss
Ancient when the world was still young.
Its fortress stands
Where relentless water beats the land
The pulse of North Atlantic ebb and flow.
The heart still beats
In tangled streets
Under iron skies that weep to see you go.
Through jetsam dross
No love is lost.
It's as freezing, burning, gone, returning
As it ever was.

And every tide and ocean swell
Every lost and tolling bell
That sings to us from deep beneath the waves
And as the ocean rolls a multitude of weary souls
Would find comfort if this field could be their grave.
Every breached and broken storm defence
Every current we must swim against
The journey we must make to find ourselves.
And as the ocean rolls a multitude of weary souls
Finds rest.

CHAPTER 14
Westpoint

' **D**ry landing' is, I suppose, relative. Better to say that we didn't have to jump into calf-deep water when going ashore at Westpoint. But dry, we were not, thanks to the boisterous disposition of the waves in this deceptively sheltered-looking part of the coast.

Climbing onto the little jetty and stepping ashore once again on my island's twin, I realised anew how marvellous the human capacity for migration is, even in the face of extreme danger. But the Falklands were purposely colonised, first by the French (yep!) then by the British. Setting out in that vast and utterly unpredictable ocean, not even knowing they were heading for *somewhere*, took more courage strength of will and mind than most of those in our safe, warm, charted, GPS-ridden world could ever hope to muster. The cynic in me seeing displayed in these islands every misery of climate (it was now raining, water from the sky, joining that from the sea which the landing craft's prow had hurled up at us) thought that had they known what they were in for, those first pioneers would have probably decided not to bother, no matter how adventurous their disposition. But these islands had only supported a population for a fraction of human history (less than 400 years). Humans have roamed the rocks and hills, peat bogs and beaches of the Outer Hebrides since before history began. What possessed those Neolithic explorers to set out into that vicious sea in their tiny boats? For Lewis, although visible from the mainland (when it's not raining but is about to rain) it's not exactly reached by the safe coastal navigation of the ancient seafarers of the Mediterranean. I ought to know, because it possesses me too.

Lewis may be less isolated geographically than the Falklands, but in terms of the power of human endeavour required to reach them, with the relative technologies of their respective eras of settlement, the two showed another similarity to add to that of their geology, meteorology and ecology.

Looking at the distribution of landmass of this great planet, Earth, the Isles that call themselves British huddle together, as though pushed away from the mainland of the Eurasia plate and driven out towards the fierce Atlantic Ocean, the very rock of our nation's geological make-up outcast from Europe.

And hanging in there, on the flip side of the equator, the same latitude south as the capital city of their motherland, this tiny knot of islands that also still call themselves British.

Humanity had spread out across that landmass, out of Eden, out of Africa, it makes no difference, and were not halted by its boundaries. The blood of those itinerant hunter-gatherers still flows in the veins of the human race. We are still a nomadic species; just some of us prefer to stay at home.

Is that why I keep travelling, on my perpetual *peregrinatio*, because I don't know where 'home' is? And if I found it, would *I* prefer to stay there? Perhaps I'm afraid of finding it in case I did, because I don't ever want to stop moving.

Trekking up the peaty hill towards the seabird colonies that were the object of the afternoon's excursion I had a strange, almost out-of-body experience. A Landrover-full of the less agile passengers (I recognised one of Arnau's 'English teachers' amongst them, peering out of the back window that was rapidly steaming up even as she wiped it with the back of her hand) passed us, transporting them the mile or so from the jetty where we had made our 'dry' landing to the cliff. We certainly weren't 'dry' anymore – what the aforementioned boisterous waves had started the rain had made complete, further perfecting the similarity between this and my own dear Outer Hebrides.

'Oh, for goodness' sake,' I said to Dad as they passed us. 'It's not exactly far.'

We had all had to have medical examinations to certify an adequate level of fitness before the voyage. They couldn't have been unfit enough to need to ride in a Landrover.

There might have been a 'Tsk! Tourists!' in my internal monologue. I had to remind myself that despite the wind and the rain, the mushy peat and the scrubby grass underfoot, here I was just as much a 'tourist' as they were.

Dad wandered off along a natural path formed between clumps of marram that soon hid him from easy view. All I could see that betrayed his location was the occasional flash of red beneath his olive beanie hat. His hat was blending in with the surrounding flora rather better than the expedition-issue parkas. After a permit yesterday to wear civvies, we were now back in uniform.

Some were more uniform than others. The suitcase debacle had meant that fifteen of our number had hurriedly purchased gear in the shop in Ushuaia, and variations on the themes of boots and walking trousers were limited. I had noticed, shortly before my disparaging mental assessment of Peggy and the others in the Landrover, Bill and Sylvia trudging up the hill wearing matching trousers and boots, as well as obligatory red parka. Identically dressed couples make me feel faintly nauseous. But this occurrence of the sickly phenomenon served to remind me once again of that less-than-ideal start to the trip and how fortunate we had been. But I decided to make a game of it – a sort of 'snap' with my fellow passengers as the cards.

There was another recurring theme that was the legacy of a Spanish airline trying to reduce the weight of their aircraft. Something that I did not expect to see now that the cost and quality of digital cameras had fallen and risen respectively such that everyone seemed to have one (even if the quality of the camera rarely seemed to rub off on the quality of the photographs). Something that saddened me. There were an awful lot of disposable cameras around. And had my suitcase been a victim of Iberian's cost-cutting measures, I'd have been using them too. I rested my hand on the case round my neck, grateful for its presence. If a bad worker is not to blame their tools, is it all right for a good worker to praise them? Not that a disposable camera is a complete hindrance. I took one of my best photographs ever on a disposable, at a rodeo in Pasadena. But to rely on them completely... I was checking myself regularly now for becoming a slave to the camera, for having my face buried in it so that I missed what was actually happening. But then I realised. When that camera is in action I am not a tourist taking holiday snaps. When the lens cap comes off I am a photographer, and my camera and I are a partnership, part of the symbiosis of human and machine that I had been aware of my whole life.

I am a trapper, like the trappers of the turn of the last century in the Canadian Arctic. My quarry moves, hides, evades – the best photographs are rarely posed-for. I am a trapper of images.

But there were some things my partner could not share.

The birds.

I knew from standing on the stern trying to shoot albatrosses – I had had considerably less luck with my camera than the Ancient Mariner, if it could have been called that in his case, had with his crossbow – that it was pointless. I would just miss it all, and not even have any good pictures to show for it.

So I stood still and watched, trying not to over balance as I tipped my head back to see as much of the sky as possible.

The birds soared through the air, landed and took off again in a cacophony of movement. I allowed myself the clichéd marvel there were no mid-air collisions, but also to note with equal admiration that there were no crashes on take off or landing when none of the birds on the ground made any effort to give way to the incoming missiles of feathers and beaks that touched down in the tightest of spaces in their midst.

God, or Nature, the choice is yours, had created aeronautical perfection in the wings of the albatross. But God had not created any sort of air traffic control. Man may have succeeded in mathematically emulating Nature, but still needed to impose order upon his creation. Nature, it seemed, did not.

Was air traffic control a further paradigm for the image of God in Man? Or of Man's desire to become as God? Man has 'created' flight, and as God exerted His will upon the chaos of the sea, Man exerts his upon his movement in the air. And just as the sea will rage and destroy, so too will airborne accidents occur when control is lost. Does the destruction and havoc wreaked by the ocean happen because God has lost control of the chaos? Surely such a thought is heretical. No, God does not lose control. He lengthens the chains. And that is the uncrossable gulf between mortal and divine – Man cannot guarantee to keep control of his chaos.

But Man's technological triumph, the object of his dreams since Daedalus sought to escape the Isle of Crete, is nothing that wasn't created an age-of-the-earth ago. Nor does it need any sort of control imposed on it from outside. As with so many things, in the comings and goings of the seabird colony there was order in the chaos. And nothing was enforcing it.

Humans naturally make a lot of noise when wrapped in Gore Tex and moving through rain and foliage (however scruffy and wind-whipped) but even so I wasn't aware of Dad returning to my side from his short foray into Westpoint Isalnd's answer to Hampton Court's maze until he tapped my shoulder.

'Amy,' he said and pointed to the clump of vegetation. 'Baby albatrosses.'

He guided me in front of him into the marram. Beyond it was an outcrop of rock that rose up above the surface of the ground like a lump on a clobbered head. It was entirely hidden from view from the open ground unless you plunged off through the marram. A few red parkas, harsh against the greens, greys and browns that the island wore indicated that some at least had found it. And of course, there were those who would think that they were special and had more right to see than anybody else. Or that their spouse had more right to see than anybody else. Such was going on near by. A man was being quite insistent with his shoulders that his wife have a grandstand view. The voices, mercifully (and surprisingly) appropriately hushed, were American. A flash of yellow among the red indicated the presence of a guide. She asked the woman to move. Both she and her husband ignored her. I squeezed forward along a different track. Being short may not get you best view of a lot of things, but it does make it easier to get into tight spaces.

Dad pointed over my shoulder at the rookery. I know a delighted smile was spreading across my face. They were beautiful. Still quite fluffy, they were more than chicks but as yet lacked the elegance and regal bearing of the adult birds. They were gawky adolescents. Even albatrosses are 'awkward teenagers'! But I knew that the clumsy youngster I was watching would soon evolve into grace given form.

And just as I, with human intellect, recognised the destiny of magnificence in those ungainly young birds, does a higher intellect than ours look at our clumsiness and bunglings and failures and know that one day we too are destined for greater beauty?

The scene set out before us was so quintessentially British that I wondered if I had wandered onto the set of a micky-taking Monty Python sketch. And to describe it makes me wonder if I am in danger of appearing to try to emulate what one might expect to find in an Enid Blyton book. (I hope I am not!)

We had been told during the pre-landing briefing that we were to visit a house on Westpoint, and been assured that we couldn't possibly mistake it. Sure enough, set back from beach and dunes was a house, the only building that we could see on this stretch of the coastline. It was quite a large house with a garden that was obviously well cared for but was wearing the dress of the southern autumn. Nearer the dune's edge a flagpole displayed southern-hemisphere patriotism, flying the Union Flag. Almost paradoxically, it didn't look at all out of place there, despite the land-and-seascape so closely resembling the Scottish Islands. Indeed, it seemed more comfortable with itself that many of its siblings displayed on the other side of the world.

After dutifully removing our boots at the door, we were directed into what I can only really call a parlour; 'Sitting room' or 'lounge' doesn't quite do it justice. In the centre was a table laden with cakes and biscuits, and on a sideboard there were large pots of tea with stacks of cups, saucers and plates. Those who had arrived before us had already made themselves at home and were sitting on a variety of chairs, stools and sofas with their hands wrapped around cups of tea, plates of cakes at their elbows.

'Good grief, but this is weird,' I breathed.

We had been told that the family who lived here opened their house to parties from the 'cruise' ships (though I say again, you won't get many true cruise ships here) and laid on afternoon tea for them, but even so, it was rather surreal. I looked round at Dad. His specs had steamed up, and he was wiping them clean for his own double-take.

In the welcoming warmth I realised just how cold I was. Gloves are not conducive to the efficient operating of cameras and mine had barely been on since our arrival at the albatross rookery. But...

'I've got to get a photo of this. No-one'll believe it.'

I fumbled at the camera case with my stinging, thawing fingers, pulled it out and removed the lens cap, very slowly, the pinch on the catches seeming to require the utmost concentration. I raised the sensitive optical instrument to my eye and watched as the English afternoon tea tableau before me became surrounded by mist. The lens was suffering in the same way Dad's specs had. I wiped it with my scarf, aware that the movement of my fingers was still slow and clumsy, and prepared for the shot again. No good. And now view through the viewfinder was completely fogged up.

'Pants, it's the mirror,' I muttered.

One of the balancing acts of thermally testing an observation satellite, when it is put in what is essentially a big freezer/oven and the temperature is cycled between very cold and very hot, is making sure that the mirror in the imager (the imager being essentially just a very big, very powerful camera) is never the coldest part of the spacecraft as the temperature rises. If this happens any debris in the chamber will adhere to it and is a right royal pain to clean off. I have spent many nightshifts monitoring the transition from cold to hot of a spacecraft under test, to prevent this happening. And here I was, falling foul of the affliction in miniature. Of course the mirror in a SLR camera is far less delicate and precise that a space-based multi-spectral imager, but the principle is the same, and I knew that when the camera had reached thermal equilibrium with its surroundings the mirror would clear itself. Sadly thermal equilibrium was not achieved while we were warming our hands around cups of tea and taking the edge of our peckishness with scones and jam (the church calendar made most of the delights on offer off limits to me, like my dessert at dinner that first night, but then I suppose that's what makes it a *discipline*) and so I have no photographic evidence of that bizarre and hospitable scene.

'No-one'll believe it,' I had said.

You'll just have to take my word for it.

Nordnorge was ploughing on into the darkness again, the open ocean in front of her, and she was happy that way. The next land fall we would make would be Buenos Aires, where the unfortunate owners of the prodigal luggage had been promised they would be reunited with it. Was it a cause for killing the fatted calf, I wondered, as they had managed very well without it. Karen-the-courier had confided to Dad, relief in her voice, that thank goodness it was the British who had lost their suitcases and not the Germans or the Americans. None of the Suitcase Owners had complained or tried to hold Norwegian Coastal Voyage responsible. She suspected that would not have been the case with either of the other two dominant nationalities on board. Ah, the stiff British upper lip. It still appears to be there even as the rest of what once made Britain great is slipping away (despite the proudly displayed colours on the flagpole at Westpoint).

Two of the Unfortunate Suitcase Owners were sitting next to us now in the Deck 4 corridor lounge. They were the Glaswegian Grannies, who I had first encountered at dinner on the first evening. I had spoken with them several times during the course of the voyage. And it made me miss my gran, and wish again and again that she was still alive, and that she was here with us.

They were discussing shopping.

For so long the ship's souvenir shop had had the monopoly, but yesterday in Stanley there had been other opportunities. Dad and I have a joke about 'hitting the shop' when we arrive in any town smaller than Stornoway. It was, of course, trotted out for Stanley.

'What did you buy?' The less-old asked the other.

'A penguin.'

I assumed she meant a cuddly toy penguin.

'What sort of penguin?'

I glanced across at Dad. He had also been distracted from his reading material, an enormous book he'd bought in the museum at Gritviken and knew he was going to regret it when it came to getting it into his suitcase and a smile was twitching at the corners of his mouth.

'A black and white one.'

He pinched the bridge of his nose just as I clamped a hand across my mouth to hold back the guffaw that had been building up the whole time I'd been ear wigging. We sat in our (hopefully) silent mirth waiting for the next instalment but the pair had fallen into the sort of companionable silence that comes when everything has been said a dozen times or more.

But it's a thing worth taking some contentment in, that something so simple had pleased Granny. It was a tonic to my natural cynicism, which had been rattling its cage a little more than I would have liked recently. Perhaps it had served me right for listening in, but there seemed to be some sort of balance in that the snarling beast awakened by one overheard conversation should be soothed, if not altogether sedated, by one. Not everyone had been as satisfied with their visit to the Falklands as the Glaswegian Grannies.

Maybe my indiscretion can be forgiven. They could probably have heard her on the bridge.

'I know I'm not a British citizen, but they could have at least x-rayed.'

The woman who had bruised her ribs back in the Drake Passage, and subsequently been passed as fit by the ship's doctor, had obviously been to visit the hospital in Stanley.

Why? I demanded in my in internal monologue. The perpetual collective arrogance of the Americans on board had finally drip-drip-dripped me into open irritation. They hadn't wanted us. The American Revolution, with the loss of the Thirteen Colonies, was such a major blow to the British Empire that historians consider it a watershed. Break away from your sovereign power then expect its subjects to treat you as a fellow citizen? And while our soldiers are out there in the Middle-East fighting your war, marching in your invasion which stinks to the firmament of imperialism...[16]

What had we created?

This monster, this spoiled brat that whined and moaned and shot things when it didn't get its own way was a child of the Empire. A child that had stormed out of the parental home in anger and violence. And yet that abused parent still sent her sons to fight its battles for it.

'We could have gone it alone,' an American soldier had reputedly said.

Well, why didn't you then? It would have meant you'd have all the glory and no-one could suggest otherwise. But then there would have been no-one to share the humiliation when it all went wrong. No, not share – shoulder the lot.

Maybe the disowned parent refused to disown the rebellious child and would not see it wanting, even if what it wanted was a hypocritical 'liberation' of another country. They didn't exactly take kindly to 'foreign' troops on 'their' soil in the late 1700's. But as the fat truck driver, over two hundred years later, munches on 'Freedom Fries'[17] he would do well to remember that ultimately it was the involvement of the French navy that won the American

---

[16] This was when the 'War on Terror' was still considered to be a legitimate concept and we had Prime Minister who... well, Maggie would have had none of it, that's for sure.

[17] 'America' (as an entity in itself, it seemed) was so incensed that France would not send troops to help them fight Saddam Hussein that they re-branded 'French Fries.' But they're not, anyway. They're called 'chips.'

War of Independence.

Can we, like Prospero, find the grace to say, 'This vile thing we acknowledge ours'?

The Imperial Trans-Antarctic Expedition, Shackleton had called it. And it wasn't really that long ago.

And it all began in the tangled branches of the Royal Family Trees of two small nations that had grown up side by side, the border shuffling north and south, like Jacob and Esau wrestling in the womb. We didn't really want each other, not since the days of Longshanks. I sometimes wonder what went on inside Good Queen Bess's head. The politics are understandable – marry and her husband takes power, name an English successor and it opens up the way for carnage (literally) in the court. But for all her grand inspiring speeches and declarations of devotion to England and to her subjects, did she not realise that when she died the King of Scotland would inherit the throne and England would cease to be an independent nation?

But thus was formed the United Kingdom of Great Britain

There are times when this nation seems more to be the Divided Kingdom. Devolution for Scotland, Wales and Northern Ireland. But the grim patriarchal patronising authority is still there - if you can't get along you won't be allowed to play together. And so the parliament at Stormont was dissolved.[18]

The final tottering of the Empire was to begin upon those emerald shores decades before Westminster began treating Ulster like a naughty child. When the Republic of Ireland was born. The severing of an island, a sundering whose shockwaves would ripple on through generations yet unborn.

As a Hiberno-Scot, my forefathers came from County Antrim, in what is now Northern Ireland. Some people hear Irish in my voice before they hear Scottish, even after five generations, and ask, am I Northern Irish or 'southern'? But Matthew Kernahan left in 1845, before partition. I'm just Irish (although I have been told that my ghost-accent is that of Belfast, not the most auditorially pleasing voice stamp of the Emerald Isle, and I've somehow ended up with it). And the Irish, like the Scots, are everywhere.

Until the 1940s, the decade that saw what could be considered to be the terminal decline of the British Empire, pink had been seen as a shade of red, a colour of power and strength. But it is also the hue that red takes on when it ages and fades, the Empire itself fading in potency alongside the colour that had once represented it on maps of the world.

Gone are the days when 'a quarter of the map was pink.'

Doesn't bother me, not really. I don't *do* pink.

---

[18] Between October 2002 and May 2007. When I made this trip, the Assembly was still suspended

CHAPTER 15
Homeward Bound

Before us now lay a further three days of open sea, the time when the little community settled into the village of ship-board life. One popular activity was to go for a walk, round and round and round Deck 5 (seven circuits made a mile), and it was a common sight in the morning when we were all at sea to spy pairs or occasional trios wrapped up to the cheekbones with hoods up passing you again and again at regular intervals. If one was also partaking of this pastime but travelling in the opposite direction it was possible to work out who was going faster by the distance between 'passing points' on successive orbits and so race one's fellow deck-walkers without them knowing it. Among these intrepid hikers were often those who had given me funny looks when I had tried out the stairwell as a potential exercise ground. It seemed to be perfectly acceptable to wander round and round in circles, but running up and down staircases was obviously quite mad.

I am, as the old cliché goes, insatiably curious. 'What is it?' does not mean 'What is it called?' It means 'What are its origins, what does it do and where does it fit into the fabric of the universe?' and, in the case of machinery, 'Can I take it apart?' (the answer to which is usually 'No.')

I was drinking it in, soaking it up, going under, breathing it, taking it into my brain as I take air into my lungs, allowing it to drown me so that I might be reborn different, assimilated into new understanding.

Why was I so fascinated? The cold that had radiated from that berg in the Arctic, that caress of cold Death that repulsed attracted. In those fleeting moments that had seemed so eternal, as it reached out to stroke my warm human flesh with tendrils of freezing air from its frozen surface we had been bound together in a terrible bond stronger than that of the most twisted forms of obsessive love. We had been bound by shackles of hatred. I wanted to know - know thine enemy - I wanted to understand it so that it could have no secrets from me, to know all about it as a lover does their beloved for the veil between love and hate is thinner than we know. Or would care to accept.

Something kept me detached from the rest of the lecture audience. I was perched on the edge of a table at the back as though I shouldn't have been there, as though I was seeking forbidden knowledge. And it was the desire for forbidden knowledge that brought about the Fall of Man.

I just wanted to *know*. Everything. Not just about the ice, but about the ocean, the atmosphere, all of history, chemistry, biology, every mathematical concept and proof, what goes on in the heart of a star and what does it sound like when it dies. Is this so wrong? How could Eve's desire for knowledge cause the Fall? 'When she saw that the tree was good for food, and a delight to the eyes, and to be desired to make one wise...'[li] Is the thirst for knowledge really to grasp at equality with God? (And is the Serpent whispering in *my* ear now?) Why would any loving deity want His people to remain in ignorance? Or did He just want them to remain in innocence? Post-Fall Humanity is warned by that wisest of ancient sages, King Solomon, of the dangers that come with learning:

'With much wisdom comes much sorrow, the more knowledge the more grief.'[lii]

Don't think about the Piri Reis Map...

The Apocryphal Old Testament considers the invention of writing an evil, taught to Man by one of the angels who fell with Lucifer. However, other sources credit Enoch with its invention, and Enoch was one of those figures who walked so closely with God that he did not die but was 'no more' because he was taken straight to Heaven, a sort of metaphysical sublimation – going straight from solid (flesh) to gas (spirit) without having to lie putrefying in the ground, a state that can be quite appropriately represented by 'liquid.'

But if to seek knowledge is considered rebellion, why is wisdom so lauded in the Scriptures?

Knowledge is knowing that a tomato is a fruit. Wisdom is knowing not to put it in a fruit salad. Knowledge without wisdom can be a dangerous thing.

Does it depend on the knowledge sought? After all, Eve sought knowledge that would make her like God. Dante recognized the human thirst for learning, the 'intellect's disquiet.'[liii] And he came to understand during his ascent into Heaven that that disquiet could be eased by 'nothing save the light of truth, God's truth, which holds all truth within its rays.'[liv]

Perhaps it is that the pursuit of knowledge and wisdom is admirable in itself, after all, Eve was taking a 'short-cut' to knowledge as the fruit would make her wise instantly, and it is this quest, this seeking, that keeps us going, keeps us striving for discovery, keeps us *exploring*. This is what made our first ancestors take that long walk out of Africa and across the surface of the Earth; this is what made ancient Man set out across the sea in their little dug-out canoes and coracles of animal skin, abandoning coastal navigation and venturing into the open ocean; this is why Cook was sent to search for *Terra Australis Incognita*. This was what drove *them*, Pierry and Amundsen, and Scott. And Nansen, the eloquent and poetic scientist, and Shackleton, the clinical and forensic poet.

Yes, I can understand why God would want mankind to remain innocent even if it risked their remaining ignorant. The innocent strive to better themselves, without the corruptions of greed and ambition, to explore for exploration's sake, to see what lies beyond the next hill or what land we'll reach if we hold this course. Maybe that's another reason why I keep travelling, retaining my innocence by keeping my keel in the ocean.

But right now, I just wanted to *know*.

ORION IS UPSIDE DOWN

What is it?

What is its genus? How do we label it, put it in a box and say we now know what it is, for it is such categorization that leads us to believe we no longer have to fear something. Is it animal, vegetable or mineral?

Ice is a mineral, a naturally occurring inorganic crystalline solid. But even then, it has fifteen known crystal structures.

And is it solid?

Ice moves.

For a moment I am back in my chemistry class. The teacher tosses a lump of something black at me and I catch it. On closer inspection, it is not black but very dark brown. It is bitumen residue, the teacher says, the most viscous constituent of crude oil. It must be solid, mustn't it? After all, you couldn't catch a liquid if someone threw it at you. Could you? I examine the object again. Although mostly uneven, one end of it has a smooth curve where it has been sitting in the jar. It's a liquid, my teacher explains, it just flows very, very slowly.

But ice is not like that.

The bitumen moulds itself to the shape of its container. Ice moulds itself to nothing. When it starts to move, nothing, not even the hardest of ancient metamorphic rock can stand in its way. Ice moulds its container, the steep sides of fjords and mountain ranges, to itself.

The bitumen moves under the influence of gravity, tugging on each molecule and gradually deforming the whole. Ice moves under the impulse of its own pressure.

At a depth of fifty metres ice will begin to undergo plastic flow.

This has nothing to do with the substance we make Biro pens and Lego bricks and cheap tat out of. This is a technical term...

And now I'm in a lecture theatre, copying the stress-strain diagrams from the blackboard. Again, here stress and strain mean something quite different from their day-to-day applications. They are governed conveniently and predictably by mathematics.

Until...

'Here!' The lecturer (he doesn't like Aeronaticals - they frequently out-perform his Mechanical students in the Engineering Materials exam) hits a point on the diagram with the end of a metre ruler. 'Here is the point of no return. Beyond this magnitude of force the metal will not return to its original shape when the force is removed. This,' he whacks the board again, 'is,' and he write the words on the abused blackboard, double underlining them, 'plastic deformation.'

But under thousands of tons of its own pressure, even assisted by components of gravity, metal does not move.

It is as though ice *decides* to move.

It is a unique state of matter.

It is a solid which flows.

Ice is not metal, but it exhibits one of its properties.

It is less dense than its liquid form.

It is the only known non-metallic substance which expands when it freezes. Many of us have had the unwelcome practical demonstration of this in the form of burst pipes in winter. And ice in a glass floats. But without this property, which other non-metallic substances do not have, natural bodies of water would freeze from the bottom up, killing off vast quantities of wildlife and vegetation every year in those parts of the hydrosphere where it exerts its influence.

Ice is... kind?

In its rebellion, its refusal to conform to what is expected of a solid, inorganic, non-metallic mineral, it allows life to continue beneath its surface in its perennial habitats.

Is it kindness merely not to end life when one has the power to do so?

But what of one thousand five hundred and twenty-three lives?

Ice has another peculiarity. When it comes into extremely forceful contact with a hard substance such as steel its crystals regroup and form pyramids, sharp points capable of puncturing metal. It actually *attacks* a ship coming into contact with it in such a way.

To refrain from killing on a whim is not mercy.

But even after all this, there was something that tugged at me, something quite simple, yet it puzzled me. When the call for questions came...

'Is there any reason why icebergs in the Arctic are blue?' And I added that I hadn't seen any blue ones here.

'There are blue bergs in the south as well,' the lecturer replied and went on to explain.

The blue is due to nitrogen in the snow that is forming the berg. As more and more oxygen is squeezed out of the ice - as it gets harder - the blue nitrogen becomes dominant. The older the ice, the more it has been compressed, the harder it is, the bluer it is.

The same chemical characteristics that give us glorious skies give the identifying hue to the hardest, oldest, cruellest icebergs.

The berg in the Arctic. Ancient. Hard. Something primal darkly seducing me with its horror.

'But they're not only blue,' the lecturer continued. 'There are green ones too.'

And ice mast-high came floating by
As green as emerald

How did Coleridge know?

I have since learned that although blue icebergs inhabit both north and

141

south polar regions, the green bergs are unique to the Antarctic.
How did he know?

There was a lecture on *Titanic* that afternoon. ('No, I'm not giving it,' I had pre-empted Dad's facetious comment when I told him about it at lunchtime.) So I wasn't the only one to see her in these ice-fields, even though they were at the wrong end of the planet. Where there is ice, there her ghost is also...

Our subsidiary which processes the images from our constellation of observation satellites had been on alert. Most of us are blissfully clueless of what goes on behind the glass wall that separates them from the rest of the company; we can see them, but few of us have much idea of what they do from day to day. They just get on with it. The regular e-mail with a link to their newsletter, which usually lies in my inbox, skimmed through but unread until it is displaced by the next one, arrived late one Friday afternoon. I opened it absently, going through the motions of paying attention to what the satellites we built actually do once they get up there. And my jaw slackened, and a lump rose in my throat.

There was a photograph of dozens of fishing boats, surrounded by ice and covered in frost. The pack had swept down the east coast of Canada from Labrador without any warning and had caught them. A hundred little ships all trapped in the ice. Our guys had been supplying data to the Canadian coastguard so that they could rescue the crews.

The tears were welling up now. I suddenly felt so proud. So proud of our tiny satellites – they're only about a metre cubed. They're simple machines, not much more than a camera that can point itself towards the Earth. Little satellites saving the crews of little ships. The number rescued could not have possibly totalled 1,523. And did a hundred little ships make up for one big ship? It was literally the tip of the iceberg. But I felt as though I had done something, even if my revenge was only to prevent it taking more lives.

...'Is there any point in you going? You're not going to pick out his every mistake?'

'It's in German.'

'So you're not going.'

Dad probably thought he was stating the obvious.

'Yes, I think I will.'

I hoped that knowing what the lecturer was talking about would help me expand my German vocabulary. I tucked myself away at the back of the room next to the door, although I think I was more conspicuous there than I would have been if I'd just parked myself in the middle of a row. I recognised the lecturer, a Norwegian fellow, and knew he spoke excellent, almost accent-less English (the middle-aged American ladies would never find any fault with him) and felt a little hard-done-by that the lecture wasn't being offered in English. Brigette had, after all, managed to cater to both linguistic groups as she expounded upon the admirable qualities of penguins.

But even in a language of which my command was, by my own admission, worse than poor I did manage to find a mistake. There was never any intention to call *Britannic* '*Gigantic*.' It was everybody's friend The Newspapers once again, commenting on the connotations of immensity in the names of White Star's new liners - '*Olympic, Titanic...* What next? *Gigantic*?'

And unfortunately, a lot of people now thought I spoke German.

CHAPTER 16
Orion is Upside Down!

'*M*idnatsol, huh? You been on her?'
My fellow passengers were reading my T-shirts again. I was wearing a polo shirt with the Hurtigrute logo, a stylised silhouette of a ship roughly conforming to *Nordnorge*'s own outline with an exaggerated red band across the hull, and 'Midnatsol' embroidered beneath it in a script designed to look like handwriting.

I was slightly surprised that anyone, especially this large American gentlemen who didn't look like he was likely to be a follower of the hard-working coastal vessels that made up the Hurtigrute fleet, should be interested in *Midnatsol*.

Midnatsol, whose name I was wearing across my chest, latterly *Midnatsol II* and now sailing under the name of *Lyngen* and soon to be *National Geographic Explorer* was a 'mid-generation ship,' which roughly translates as 'old enough to be annoying but not old enough to be interesting.' Indeed, this is the same ship I mentioned earlier as a victim of the ugly stick. These 'mid-generation ships' might not have been graced with beauty, but they were of approximately the same vintage as our old ferry, *Suilven*, who was herself built in Norway. Old *Suilven*'s departure for New Zealand when she was replaced with the not-terribly-imaginatively named *Isle of Lewis* on the Stornoway run was the first time I had found myself rent from a ship I loved dearly and had been a part of my life for years knowing I was unlikely to ever see her again. The next would be the *QE2*. But for the sake of *Suilven*'s memory I had a soft spot for these overgrown floating shoe-boxes. Even *Narvik*, a thoroughly miserable vessel, with no soul whatsoever, and everybody said so, even her crew, I refused to give up on. Actually, *Narvik*, by then sold and sailing as *Gann*, became one of the heroes of the ash cloud, when for over a week in April 2010 ash from an erupting volcano with an unpronounceable name in Iceland grounded every aeroplane in Britain. She was chartered and brought back fifty or so Britons who had got stranded on the continent and had congregated in Bergen, then returning about ninety mainland Europeans to the continent. I confess to being a little sanctimonious in the aftermath of the ash cloud even if I did get caught in it. I was in Belfast, attending as I do every year the *Titanic* Memorial Ceremony and was due to fly back to London. I think there's some kind of cosmic justice there. I had travelled there to honour the memory of a ship and yet I had flown there. It seems a fitting irony that I should fall victim to the logistical carnage when air travel was suddenly halted. I could hear her ticking me off - *serves you right. Now, get yourself down the docks.* A lot had changed since I had last been to the docks and I found what I recognised as the Stena Terminal to be deserted and boarded up, the eeriness being added to by this being five o'clock in the morning. I was naive enough to ask a watchman at the Isle of Man Steam Packet terminal where the terminal now was and think he'd tell me, but he just kept unhelpfully repeating, 'Ye've a helluva walk.' I didn't care - I just needed to know which direction to walk in. The sun was rising when I reached the new terminal building, I'd found a happily unpatronising taxi driver on the outskirts of the city, but it was mid afternoon when I finally got a place on a ship. Walking up the linkspan boarding her I turned around and saluted Queen's Island, where Harland and Wolff had once held court, where *Titanic* had been built, where countless magnificent ships had been built – indeed when I had begun making my annual pilgrimage the yard had still been functioning, I had witnessed its decline year upon year with each visit – now desolate. A spectrum of emotion tore through my heart. Sadness that the proud ship-building history of this wonderful city, for Belfast is wonderful, with a beauty crowned in thorns, should be over, and the decayed ocular proof lay before me. Anger that the ships that had begun their lives here, here and in a score of other yards like it, had been made obsolete, ocean liners replaced by airliners. And triumph that the upstart had been brought to its knees and now it was that which it had usurped which was bringing the people it had stranded home. Vive le ship! Samson and Goliath, the two enormous gantry cranes that are all that is left of Harland and Wolff, gazed down upon the scene, perhaps too old and tired to care, but I hoped they might have taken some pride in knowing that the departed era to which they belonged was superior to the modern times which had taken its place.

'Yes, I've been on her,' I said answering the American gentleman's question about *Midnatsol.*

We had boarded her in port on one of our voyages on the Hurtigrute. It had been shortly before she was to be sold and it was a sort of farewell visit, as we knew we wouldn't see her again. Well, thought we knew. After she was sold and renamed *Lyngen* the Hurtigrute continued to charter her when their own ships were off doing crazy things in places like the Antarctic.

'Is it a nice ship?'

'Well, yes...' I was a bit bemused. Like I've intimated, this ship wasn't really anything to get excited about unless you were an enthusiast. Then it dawned on me...

'Oh, that *Midnatsol*!'

He was referring to one of the new ships, very new ships, that had recently entered service. And... oh, dear...

'Yes, I've been on her too.'

And it had wrung my heart.

The *Midnatsol* whose name I wore across my chest had one kind of ugliness. It was a functional ugliness, like the ugliness of concrete. She was a working ship and was designed and built to work and it really didn't matter if she looked like she'd been drawn with a ruler and a set-square. Her aesthetics, or lack of same, had no effect on her ability to get passengers from A to B, to deliver food, window frames or wicker chairs to the isolated northern towns or to carry the mail. The *Midnatsol* that had interested the American gentleman had another kind of ugliness, the ugliness of the cruise ship, the ugliness of 'here's a hotel, make it float.' Two ugly ships, with their affliction due to their being at opposite ends of a scale. One was ugly because she worked, the other because she was a thing of leisure.

Midnatsol and her sister *Trollfjord*, who was launched on my twenty-second birthday so I feel an attachment to her despite it all, were two of the biggest mistakes the Hurtigrute has made in recent years. Attempting to cater to the 'cruise' market, they had built cruise ships. But the Coastal Voyage is not a cruise - it is a voyage, the genuine public transport of the Long Coast, and these enormous ships designed to carry German tourists in summer were having to scrape by carrying sometimes less than ten passengers in the winter, unable to take enough in fares to pay for their own fuel.

I will tear down my barns and build bigger ones...[lv]

'Well, if you want a floating hotel...'

But the American gentleman had wandered on. Why ask the question if you're not going to wait for the answer?

'Amy, the skies are clear.'

Dad had one hand on the back of my chair and leaned in to deliver the news almost right into my ear, as though it were a secret to be guarded, to be kept just between ourselves for as long as possible, like Elephant Island. Or maybe it was because he knew that this was something I had been longing for since our arrival in the southern hemisphere and he was enjoying telling me that it was here.

While my friends had been joining dots on paper I had been joining dots in the sky. The night skies above Lewis are still dark, even as the rest of the country slowly becomes engulfed in a universal orange glow. Since I left, I have hardly ever seen the stars. They called to me, the little girl lying flat on her back in the garden gazing up into the deep – I had accepted that running away to sea on a tea clipper wasn't really a career option – and to answer that call I have had to leave them behind. From our Mission Control Centre in Guildford I have watched six satellites I have worked on achieve orbit, but I don't see the stars anymore.

I have always loved maps of the sky as much as I love maps of the oceans, the beautiful, intricate depictions of the constellations formed from only a few bright stars. Looking at these, how could Ursa Major be anything other than a bear, Cassiopeia anything other than a queen upon her throne? How could Orion be anything other than a mighty hunter?

They had all been the faithful companions of northern mariners since the ancients first set out in their coracles. But they are fixed in their spheres and could not follow as the pioneers sailed south. As they crossed the Line, the task of guiding storm-tossed, star-crossed sailors was passed to their companions beyond the southern horizon. Cetus the Whale, the Southern Cross, Hydra the Sea Monster, not lurking in the deep to devour them but stretching across the sky to guide them.

I had never seen them. But I had studied their images. They were mysterious, mythical within mythology, the Here-There-Be-Monsters of the heavens; they were just beyond reach. And among them, there is a Ship, *Argo Navis*. No longer an 'official' constellation (who decides these things anyway?) she has been broken up by astronomical ship-breakers, and is now the Keel, the Stern and the Sail. Her Mast has become the *Pyxir Navis*, the Ship's Compass. Is that *my* compass? A ship sails the heavens – might it be *her*? – and was one of the inevitabilities of my life that I should seek her?

We clattered up the stairs to the weather deck and sternwards, away from the ship's running lights. Suddenly we were back in our house in Stornoway, on a clear and cold winter's night. The telescope that Dad had bought me for my sixteenth birthday, a 60mm refractor the colour of orange juice, was standing a little precariously on its tripod in the back garden trained on a large, bright star that did not twinkle. I burst into the living room.

'Dad! I've seen the moons of Jupiter!'

He put down his book and got up – I didn't need to say, 'Come and see!' – and, still in his shirtsleeves, followed me out. I proudly showed him my 'discovery' and he peered through the eyepiece taking great care, as I had warned him, not to touch the tripod.

'Oh, yes,' he said, the same delight and wonder in his voice as I had felt when I focused the precious optical instrument on the object which according to the sky charts in the current issue of *Astronomy Now* was Jupiter and had seen…

'A disc, and four little dots across the middle. I can see it!'

He was seeing what Galileo had seen at almost four hundred years ago, the discovery that had changed the scientific and theological worlds completely. The discovery that the Earth was not the centre of the Universe, that not all celestial objects orbited it. The centre of the Universe for these four tiny pin-pricks of light was Jupiter. And it was a humbling thought that my little telescope had let me see what Galileo had seen and had changed our view of the cosmos forever.

The European Navigation Satellite Constellation is to be called Galileo. My first satellite was its prototype, and its name is *Giove*, Italian for Jupiter.

Now, here on board *Nordnorge*, out on the Southern Ocean, Dad was showing me the sky. What would I see there, what would I be able to point out to him? What would I recognise...?

Nothing.

Or so it seemed.

I gazed upwards in astonishment and awe. Nothing above me was familiar. I stood beneath a sky that was utterly alien to me. I had been navigating by the stars since I was a teenager but here, suddenly, I was lost. It was this – not the silent sentinels of ice in the water nor the blankets of it that covered the land, not the strange and wonderful creatures that made this their home – that made me realise how far away I was; how far away I was... from *my* home. There is ice in the north, not far from the latitudes in which I grew up. The landscape of the Earth is mirrored across the Equator. But not the cosmos, for the Earth, as Galileo found, is not at its centre, and is among that magnificence rather insignificant. And amazing. And wonderful.

'What is man that Thou art mindful of him?' asked the Psalmist. 'The son of man that Thou visitest him?'

For the Creator to take notice of so tiny a speck in such vastness of glory, we must be special to Him indeed.

'[He] maketh Arcturus, Orion, and Pleiades, and the chambers of the south.'[lvi]

Arcturus is the Great Bear. And the 'chambers' or constellations of the south, that ancient Hebrew poet knew they were there although he could not see them.

And now I could.

I continued to search the sky, more and more stars appearing as my eyes adjusted, as though they were coming out to play.

Hello! Here we are! Here we are!

And they just kept coming, until the mass of fainter stars began to obscure the brighter ones I had been searching to try to find those mystical constellations I had only ever seen on star charts. No Bears were to be found here, but instead there was a Centaur, a Phoenix and a Unicorn. 'Oh widowed world beneath the northern Plough, forever famished of the sight of them!'[lvii]

Unlike Dante, who newly escaped from Hell looked towards 'that alien pole and beheld four stars'[lviii] I couldn't find the Southern Cross. And I couldn't find the Ship, the celestial entity which I could easily have believed had called me here. But as I swept my gaze towards the northern horizon my eyes picked out something that seemed familiar...

I laughed, attracting looks of 'Aww, bless!' from a couple of other star gazers (as the youngest on the ship I had been adopted as a sort of mascot by some of the older passengers) and ran across the deck to where Dad was still gazing south.

'Dad!' I cried, grabbing his arm, swinging him round and pointing. 'Orion is upside down!'

CHAPTER 17
Landfalls and Departures...

The final day at sea began with Divine Service. Announced discreetly on the same notice board that had lamented the loss of a lens cap, advertised for bridge players and satirised the penguins' disappointment at our failure to land in Fortuna Bay, it appeared to have been the ship's doctor who organised it. We met in the forward bar, which on this voyage had served as lecture theatre, briefing room and now a church, and the service was taken by one of the passengers; an American pastor had been conveniently found on the ship's manifest. Services at sea, a great maritime tradition, are taken by the Captain on British ships. I wondered if there was no such tradition on Norwegian ships, or if Captain Hansen had deferred to the ordained Minister of Religion.

A week had passed since that morning on South Georgia, at Stromness, where Dad and I had taken our solitary communion. And now we sat surrounded by others of our faith. I hadn't thought about it, as I mused upon creation and sin and God in this oceanic wilderness. Had any of them being doing likewise? In a place where I had been so alone, and, yes, revelled in the martyrdom of loneliness, was I no longer alone? Had any of them pondered at the same immensities that had been crowding themselves into the book and volume of my brain since I first set foot upon this ship of souls?

A week had passed since we had stood in that place where Shackleton and his men had felt the presence of the Fourth Man. A week since the presence which had been by my side through that land of ice and snow had remained behind.

Virgil had handed me over to my Beatrice.

Dante, weep not for Virgil's going.

It's time to go home, she'd said.

I stand on air, save for the few millimetres of steel spike protruding from the cage encasing the toe-box and soles of my boots. Those spikes are all that are holding me to the wall of ice which radiates its cold against my face in a mocking caress so similar to that which enveloped me once before, oh, it seems like so long ago, in a tiny inflatable boat in a fjord on Svalbard. Except now my skin is only centimetres away. It has not had to reach out far. It has already crumbled around my crampons once, sending me sliding down the ice face and swinging away from it before my belay line caught the slack. It had thrown me off, I who had torn away chunks of its cold, hard mineral flesh, a wounded beast trying to rid itself of its attacker. Or to swat away the insect crawling upon its skin. My hands are resting only lightly on my axes, and all my weight is acting straight down through my legs. I become aware of my body, the bones in my legs, my thighs, my femurs, the flesh and blood that's wrapped around them, muscle and sinew, quadriceps and hamstrings; pelvis, shoulders, latimus dorsae and my spine, each disc and vertebra... I am balanced here, perfectly, standing on the face of this wall of ice. It fills my senses and even as I am at war with it, I am as one with it.

'Amy, up or down?' my instructor calls to me.

I have been stationary almost a minute, a long time when you are standing on a vertical ice-face. What will I see from the top? The courtyard of Somerset House with its per annual ice rink. A few rooftops on the Strand. It is tame ice, bred in captivity. I have climbed higher than most of those who have paid their £40 for the privilege and there are fewer ready-made niches into which I can sink my crampons or hook my axes. For each step I now advanced up the ice wall I had to drive into it, sending splinters tumbling to the ground beneath, my raging emotions seamless with the physical attack as I wrestled with my nemesis. I stood against its utter indifference. And so I had stopped.

'Up or down?'

'Down,' I call back. 'I'm coming down.'

'The good news is there's guacamole. The bad news is it's going to rain.'
Or:
'Thegoodnewsisthere'sguacamole.   Thebadnewsisit'sgoingtorain.'
Peggy, who hailed from the Deep American South, had a distinctive way of speaking. She allocated the expected amount of time to each sentence required to articulate it at what could be considered a normal tempo but squeezed up all the words at the beginning of that allocation and so leaving a long gap between the end of that sentence and the beginning of the next one.

I didn't really think that the provision of an avocado-based condiment would make up for it raining on the barbeque that was being held on the weather deck to mark our final day at sea (I prefer salsa anyway), but so far it hadn't rained. Quite the opposite. I had managed to get silly-sunburn, an irritating stripe by my right ear like a little red sideburn, marking the bit that I missed because I was trying to avoid getting sun-block in my hair. I had, however, remembered to plaster my ears themselves with the stuff, and I was glad that I had.

It was windy on deck, and those who had decided to sit down were holding their paper plates to the table while the food blew away anyway or had folded their plates over to make receptacles which reminded me of the pokes we used to get chips in from the chip shop above which Thomas MacLeod had lived as a lad. I didn't bother with a plate at all. I didn't want salad or tortilla chips, not even to dip in the revered guacamole; I'd just asked the chef to stick a chicken breast in a burger bun. Standing in the whipping wind trying to pretend that it was like a day on the beach and that I was actually enjoying avoiding direct hits from air-borne food and watching paper plates skid around all over the place didn't appeal. It reminded me of Sunday School picnics, when the weather wasn't quite bad enough to justify abandoning and all the children stood around shivering, determined to have a good time, 'You WILL have a good time!' oozing out of the grownups in unspoken waves.

The party could continue without me.

I wandered down to the promenade deck and took my place on the starboard side, looking northwards, towards the sun. And then out towards the horizon, a horizon that had been empty for so long I saw them - ships. Dozens, scores of ships, coming into view one by one out of the heat haze, all of them heading east, up the vast estuary of the River Plate towards Buenos Aires. The mighty Thames Estuary was suddenly tamed, grown small. This was no naval battlefield now but a joyful congregation, a migration of vessels meeting here and running on together towards their common destination. Like *Nordnorge*, many of them had been alone so long, away from the company of their own kind. And they rejoiced. Of one mind and one course, they charged onward as a mass, many individuals but a single entity, the whole so much more than the sum of its parts. This was a Fleet. So many vessels, so many species of ship - tankers and container ships and fishing boats - but here in this final stretch towards their goal, where the ocean met the river, they were one.

There is neither Jew nor Greek, male nor female; neither freeman nor slave wrote St Paul to the Galatians.

Isn't the final journey of the human soul associated with a river, crossing the Jordan?

Her courtesy and house flags beating out a triumphal tattoo, *Nordnorge* laughed.

And I laughed with her.

CHAPTER 18
...Leaving Home, Coming Home

From on deck, beneath the same lifeboat under which I had futilely sought shelter from the atmosphere-suspended waters around Cape Horn, I watched Tomas come back aboard the ship after seeing to some of the matters associated with the berthing of the ship and the disembarkation of her passengers here in Buenos Aires where the South American leg of our journey had begun over two weeks ago.

While we had been spared the ordeal of losing our luggage, ours was quite bent on giving us trouble. Dad's new suitcase, purchased after much careful inspection during our first visit to Buenos Aires, had broken as well.

Once again, Buenos Aires was *hot*. I imagined that *Nordnorge* would be glad to get back to the Norwegian Sea, cool even in the approaching northern summer. This voyage had been a one-off for passengers. It was her positioning voyage to take her back to Norway. Her Antarctic 'cruise' usually ran from Puerto Montt to Punta Arenas, across the Drake Passage and down the Peninsula as far as possible then returning to Ushuaia (or the other way round). Elephant Island, South Georgia and the Falklands weren't usually on offer, at least not by Norwegian Coastal Voyage.

Next year she would be joined by (and come to the rescue of) her sister *Nordkapp*. And soon little *Fram* would arrive. A close encounter with the snout of a glacier would send her limping back to Ushuaia on one occasion. Along with the loss of *Explorer* in late 2007 it's quite clear that although these waters have opened up to the cruise market, they have not been tamed and remain as dangerous as when iron men in wooden ships of three hundred tons and less under a spread of canvas did battle with them a hundred, a hundred and fifty, two hundred years ago. The ocean will not be pacified because someone might sue.

Disembarking the ship hadn't been the emotional experience that it was leaving *Nordkapp* that first time I had sailed on these sturdy, hardworking vessels that were natives of the Norwegian coast, because I knew I would see her again someday. There were some passengers who had stayed with the ship, and would sail right across the Atlantic, South and North, back to Norway. The voyage had been advertised as 'from the most southerly town in the world (Ushuaia – OK, the voyage was via the Antarctic Peninsula) to the most northerly' (Hammerfest). I was envious, of course. My cynical hat had crept out of my luggage and onto my head. Did those making the voyage have any appreciation for what they were undertaking, the place that such a voyage has in the history of seafaring? Or were they trophy hunters?

Yes, I was envious. Especially as we were about to 'cheat.' We were on a bus bound for Buenos Aires Airport.

And from there, Madrid Airport. It was silly o'clock in the morning, rather than silly o'clock at night this time. And this time, nothing had gone wrong. Well, we were still to reclaim the cases, hopefully at Heathrow, Dad's once again in a shocking condition with no axle and the handle beginning to shear off the last time we had seen it. We had decided that to get it from the railway station at Guildford to my flat (which fortunately was less than ten minutes' walk away) I would go home leaving Dad with his hamstrung monster, get my skateboard, which hadn't seen much action since I turned twenty, and trundle it home on that. Then it would be suitcase-shopping time again so Dad could get his gear back to Stornoway. But at least we knew what '£' meant, and the value of it. What we had thought was three hundred US dollars turned out to be three hundred pesos - about twenty quid. Yes, you get what you pay for.

I sat up straighter and looked around. The airport was decked out in its 'This is not a time to be awake' lighting. I'd become aware of people standing behind me, three or four perhaps, but I wasn't sure if they'd just arrived or if they been there for a while. I peeped over my shoulder. And then I saw it. Wrapped up in corrugated cardboard from its fine, exquisite cheek bones which peeped out to its no-doubt equally elegantly carved hooves...

'Dad,' I whispered, tugging gently on his sleeve.

'What?' He had been dozing, I think, and was a little annoyed at being disturbed.

'Look.' And I pointed over my shoulder.

And there it was... the Six Foot Wooden Giraffe of Madrid Airport.

I've learned not to say 'I'll never be back here,' because none of us knows what awaits us beyond a horizon that may seem empty and unbroken. You don't know when you'll find yourself back someplace so far away, so distant that you never thought you'd be again, even somewhere like South Georgia, the Antarctic Peninsula, Cape Horn. Seems like I've joined quite an exclusive club there these days. What was it Captain Baines of the Onedin Line said of the Panama Canal and its effect on the future of ocean travel?

'That would be the end of rounding the Horn... and when that happens, no more real men, just milksops. Canal sailors.'[lix]

So can I now call myself a true sailor?

Not only have I been round the Horn but round it the hard way, going from east to west.

I'm bound for Californ-i-a
By way of stormy Cape Horn...

That's the second verse of *The Leaving of Liverpool*, which never seems to make it into recorded versions.

The last Master of the QE2's only regret was that he had never rounded the Horn. But if that Queen's heir and successor is ever to sail from the Atlantic to the Pacific she will have to. For the second Cunard ship to bear the name Queen Mary is too long for the locks on the Canal, at least until they are lengthened, an operation already underway. As ships grow larger, the ocean will become large again, must become large again. The symbiosis evolves such that the ocean always has the upper hand. Ships were small and the ocean was cheated, both at Panama and Suez. But ships have out-grown those back streets and so with these new leviathans (Mary is three *Titanic*s plus *Nordnorge* in tonnage) the ocean becomes the ocean again, and they are certainly up to its challenges.

The luggage-less half of the British contingent had finally been reunited with their suitcases in a warehouse on the quay at Buenos Aires. They had missed an adventure of thousands of miles, but in the end their owners had managed without them and their contents. It prodded into being in my mind the question, what do we really need to be content? I thought of Bill and Sylvia in their embarrassingly matching gear, matching only because choice was rather limited in the single shop in Ushuaia, content to wash their underwear in the basin in their cabin every night. And even though the ship's on-board shop did a roaring trade in disposable cameras, do we really need to try to take what we've seen home with us? The ice and the ocean, the glaciers, the bergs and forbidding-welcoming coastlines, the whales and penguins and seals would still have been as magnificent and awesome if I had not captured those moments in a chemical process lasting one five-hundredth of a second. The healthy human retina is just as good a receptor of light and the images that it forms as the film or CCD at the focus of a camera's lens.
And this is a photographer writing.
But I know that I am not eloquent enough to be able to describe it all, not adequately. The weaver of words must rely heavily on the trapper of images. And so I am what I am, photographer-writer or writer-photographer, in the hope that what I lack in one I may make up for in the other. Or maybe I'm just a traveller, because all that I have told within these pages I would have experienced even if I had not written it all down or brought it back on twelve spools of 35mm film. But it was such an experience that it felt a little selfish to keep it to myself.

***

God's providence is our inheritance.
The mural carrying the motto, three-dimensional, vital, organic, emerges from the wall of the Island Star Chinese takeaway, next to the Royal British

Legion on the edge of Stornoway town centre.

It depicts the sea.

Lews Castle, perched on the edge of it, built by Sir Thomas Matheson as a stately home rather than for defence. (The ruins of the original Castle, stronghold of the MacLeods of Lewis, are underneath Number 1 Pier and do not feature here.) Then the ferry terminal, its design based on the old fish market now long gone. And our dear old ferry herself, bearing the name of the island she serves and proudly wearing her black and red funnel livery; black and red, like Cunard – Caledonian MacBrayne, the Cunard of the north of Scotland, and indeed the two shipping lines have a common origin.

In her offing are an old herring boat, with her fore-and-aft rig and rust-coloured sail and a modern yacht, separated by decades of history but sailing here side by side.

Leading this little parade of ships is a fishing boat, her registration number readable, SY357. It seems fitting that this small, humble vessel should lead and the big passenger ship bring up the rear, in her own characteristic humility.

And then there are the fish, waiting to be caught; staple to the economy of this island for so long, even if those days are past now and that economy, like everything else, is changing.

Said T.S. Eliot:

"We shall not cease from exploration, and the end of our exploring will be to arrive where we started and know the place for the very first time."

Perhaps it is a cliché to draw the conclusion that we can wander the earth looking for a place to call home and find that 'home' is the place we left behind. And perhaps it is also a cliché to use that particular quotation. But things become clichés because they are true, and so keep recurring until they melt into overuse.

In the mirror of the equator, the Isle of Lewis may gaze upon two might-have-beens: one, bowed beneath perennial ice, hostile by nature to any that would make it home; the other wearing the mine-field legacy of a long-ago war, made hostile to those who have made it home by human aggressors from another land.

God's providence is our inheritance. God's providence is from the sea. Our inheritance is the sea.

My inheritance is the sea.

I am of this island, and the sea provides for this island. The sea is everything. The ocean is all. All that I am.

The child captivated by the grainy images in pools of feeble light from two and a half miles below the surface of the Atlantic Ocean.

The little girl on tip-toe watching the perpetual forward-and-back, forward-and-back of a paddle steamer's pistons.

The kid in the coffee shop dreaming of the China fleet.

The young woman standing by, mesmerised, as immense, brand-new Rolls Royce engines turn over and over in a 165-year-old hull, in her heart a cocktail of joy and sorrow that this ship should be given such a gift, yet those engines will never propel her though the water.

My *peregrinatio* continues.

No, Mr Eliot. I'm not done exploring yet.

...What I ha' seen since ocean steam began
Leaves me no doot for the machine: but what about the man?
The man that counts, wi' all his runs, one million miles o' sea:
Four times the span from earth to moon... How far, Oh Lord, from Thee?[ix]

Yes. The sea is our inheritance.

Even where Orion is upside down.

EPILOGUE
Royal Geographical Society, London, February 2009

Approaching the buildings of the Royal Geographical Society from Kensington Gore, the effigy stands in an alcove in the wall, the simple legend beneath it: Shackleton. Nothing more is required. The pavement is busy and I step towards the kerb, beneath a young tree that is being nurtured there, protected by metal hoops around its trunk, so that I can stop and look up without getting in anyone's way. I discreetly touch the brim of my hat, conscious that anyone seeing me might think me a little odd. They probably didn't notice the statue recessed unobtrusively up there just above the eye-line. Come to think of it, they probably didn't notice me.

The statue was paid for by contributions from the public. In the Map Room, where I sit in a corner invisibly eating my lunch, is a maquette for another statue. That statue was never made. There was no money to commission a sculptor. The subject is Robert Falcon Scott.

It is a privilege to be here.

Those who've walked these halls before me... Among them... I suppose I should be used to it by now - being where he's been, standing where he's stood - but I'm not. And I hope I never do get used to it. When such a thing becomes routine for me, I fear I will have forfeit a little of my soul.

I hear the voice of the movie version of James Caird (the only one I know) 'This is the Royal Geographical Society, not the Royal Antarctic Society,' in my mind's ear at random intervals and each time it makes me smile.

Now I am standing in the library, below the Society building. Various artifacts from the Heroic Age of polar exploration are on display. They lie on a large table, exposed, none are in cases. Like her bell.

'Did he actually wear it?' the chap standing next to me asks.

He is referring to a Burberry helmet, lying on the table with the other artifacts.

'Yes,' the curator replies.

'Woa.' It's not sarcasm; it's genuine appreciation.

I look down at the helmet as well. He's written something on it. No cameras are permitted in here, and my notebook is in a locker outside, with all my other personal effects, and not for the first time I chastise myself for not bringing it in. So I take it with me the only way I can: I memorize it.

To Frank Thornton,
I give this helmet though it is not of any use in his combat in "When Knights Were Bold" it may be liked as it was worn "when nights were cold" when the most southerly point in this world was reached by man.
With kindest wishes
From
E. H. Shackleton

Or 'When knights were cold'? No. The knighthood was awarded after his Furthest South. He'd been just 'Ernest' then. Ah, the importance of being Ernest. It makes poor recompense for the linearity of time denying me my earlier desired wordplay, and I'm probably not the first to try that particular sprig of wit, but I couldn't resist. Incidentally, the name derives from Old High German, *eornost* meaning 'serious business' or (according to the *Oxford Dictionary of First Names*) 'battle to the death.' Certainly a fitting name for a man such as he. Perhaps there is greater importance in being Ernest than in just being earnest.

The fellow who asked about the helmet has moved on a bit. There's no-one near me on this side of the table. No-one's told us not to...

I brush my fingers over the fabric of the helmet, at the rim where it would have met with the cheek of the wearer. The same fingers that had once touched the cold brass of *Titanic*'s bell.

Had it been inevitable, this journey of mine, the ghost meeting with the demons as the machine travelled through the cryosphere? Could the former have taken place without the latter? Why seek out what most frightens you unless it is the knowledge that without a literal encounter with the corporeal there can be no slaying of the discarnate demons?

'It must take great courage to return to a place where one has suffered so much.'[lxi] Whether Lady Stancomb-Wills every really said that to Shackleton while he knelt on the floor pretending that a scone was the South Pole or not is immaterial. I have been in fear and loathing of the destructive power of ice my entire life, so what drew me to a place that is held eternally in its grip?

> What I aspired to be
> And was not, comforts me
> A brute I might have been but would not sink i' the scale

Thus responded Movie Shackleton, who looked like Kenneth Branagh, to Lady Stancomb-Wills.

But the lines immediately preceding those in Robert Browning's *Rabbi-Ben-Ezra* run as follows, and would become a truer anthem for the polar explorer who would achieve more in his failure than most do in their success:

> For thence a paradox
> Which comforts as it mocks
> Should life succeed wherein it seems to fail...

I have learned that when we have failed, when there is nothing left, when everything has been stripped away, that is when the miracles happen. They step in to fill the empty space left by hope. But if that space is not vacant, the miracles have nowhere to go.

> 'When disaster strikes and all hope is gone...'

You know how it completes.

Dante's hell had ice at its very centre. But his earthly paradise was to be found atop a mountain in the southern hemisphere on a landmass covering the polar regions. Hell and Eden one and the same. I have found that it is possible to enter a place surrounded by your worst nightmare and yet find perfect peace.

Notes

Chapter 10 Interlude: all italicised lines of poetry are from *If* by Rudyard Kipling

[i] Revelation 13:1-2

[ii] Dante, *Inferno III,* 9 as generally understood (or, I don't know exactly which translation). Dorothy L. Sayers' translation has 'Lay down all hope, you that go in by me.'

[iii] Originally Sir Edmund Hillary, although there have been many variations. This is a deliberate 'misquote' as I'm actually quoting Kenneth Branagh, who got it a little bit wrong. But the over-all meaning is the same.

[iv] Dante, *Inferno* II, 139-140, tr. Dorothy L. Sayers

[v] Dante, *Inferno* II, 142 tr. Dorothy L. Sayers

[vi] John 3:8, NIV

[vii] Job 1:19

[viii] Matthew 7:11

[ix] Matthew 7:7

[x] Revelation 21:1

[xi] John Milton, *Paradise Lost*

[xii] Genesis 1:5 - 9

[xiii] Genesis 1:2

[xiv] Dante, *Inferno* I, 2, tr. Dorothy L. Sayers

[xv] Revelation 15:2

[xvi] Dante, *Inferno* II, 6, tr. Dorothy L. Sayers

[xvii] Dante, *Inferno* VIII, 90 tr Dorothy L. Sayers

[xviii] Dante, *Inferno* VIII, 83 tr. Dorothy L. Sayers

[xix] Dante, *Paradiso* I, 149-150 tr. Dorothy L. Sayers

[xx] Dante, *Paradiso* I, 151 tr. Dorothy L.Sayers

[xxi] Dante, *Paradiso* I, 53-4 tr. Dorothy L.Sayers

[xxii] Psalm 69:34

[xxiii] Rudyard Kipling, *McAndrew's Hymn*

[xxiv] Dante, Inferno VIII, 114 tr. Dorothy L. Sayers

[xxv] Rudyard Kipling, *McAndrew's Hymn*

[xxvi] Dante, *Inferno* XXXIV, 121 tr. Dorothy L. Sayers

[xxvii] Mount Purgatory (Dante, *Inferno* XXXIV, 125 tr. Dorothy L. Sayers)

[xxviii] Dante, *Inferno* XXXIV, 125 tr. Dorothy L. Sayers

[xxix] Dante, *Prugatorio* I, 1,3 tr. Dorothy L. Sayers

[xxx] Revelation 9:6

[xxxi] Hamlet, Act V, Scene ii

[xxxii] Captain Oates, before leaving the tent to die in the blizzard.

[xxxiii] Alfred, Lord Tennyson , *All Things Must Die*

[xxxiv] Dante, *Paradiso* II, 3 tr. Dorothy L .Sayers

[xxxv] Dante, *Paradiso* II, 1 tr. Dorothy L. Sayers

[xxxvi] Dante, *Paradiso* II, 5 tr. Dorothy L. Sayers
[xxxvii] Dante, *Paradiso* II, 4 tr. Dorothy L. Sayers
[xxxviii] Dante, *Paradiso* II, 9 tr. Dorothy L. Sayers
[xxxix] Dante, *Paradiso* II, 7 tr. Dorothy L. Sayers
[xl] Dante, *Purgatorio* V, 105-108, tr.Henry Longfellow
[xli] Dante, *Purgatorio* I, 44 tr. Dorothy L. Sayers
[xlii] Dante, *Purgatorio* I, 52 – 54 tr. Dorothy L. Sayers
[xliii] Dante, *Purgatorio* XXX, 39, 41-42 tr. Dorothy L. Sayers
[xliv] Dante, *Paradiso* I, 51 tr. Dorothy L. Sayers
[xlv] The Onedin Line, 'Mutiny'
[xlvi] Dante, *Paradiso* XXIII, 70-72 tr. Dorothy L. Sayers
[xlvii] Dante, *Paradiso* XVIII, 21 tr. Dorothy L. Sayers
[xlviii] Dante, *Purgatorio* I, 31 tr. Dorothy L. Sayers
[xlix] Dante, *Purgatorio* I, 33 tr. Dorothy L. Sayers
[l] Matthew 10:29
[li] Genesis 3:6
[lii] Ecclesiastes 1:18
[liii] Dante, *Paradiso* IV, 125 tr. Dorothy L. Sayers
[liv] Dante, *Paradiso* IV, 124/126 tr. Dorothy L. Sayers
[lv] Luke 12:18
[lvi] Job 9:9
[lvii] Dante, *Purgatorio* I, 26, 27 tr. Dorothy L. Sayers
[lviii] Dante, *Purgatorio* I, 23 tr. Dorothy L. Sayers
[lix] *The Onedin Line* 'No Smoke Without Fire'
[lx] MacAndrew's Hymn, Rudyard Kipling
[lxi] Janice Stancomb-Wills, in the script of Channel Four's Shackleton

Lightning Source UK Ltd.
Milton Keynes UK
177372UK00001B/14/P

9 781906 791759